AS/A-Level ... Guide

Robert Swan

Series Editor: Marian Cox

Spies

Michael Frayn

Philip Allan Updates
Market Place
Deddington
Oxfordshire
OX15 0SE

Orders
Bookpoint Ltd, 130 Milton Park, Abingdon, Oxfordshire, OX14 4SB
tel: 01235 827720
fax: 01235 400454
e-mail: uk.orders@bookpoint.co.uk
Lines are open 9.00 a.m.–5.00 p.m., Monday to Saturday, with a 24-hour message
answering service. You can also order through the Philip Allan Updates website:
www.philipallan.co.uk

© Philip Allan Updates 2006

ISBN 978-1-84489-606-6

Printed in Malta

Philip Allan Updates' policy is to use papers that are natural, renewable and
recyclable products and made from wood grown in sustainable forests. The logging
and manufacturing processes are expected to conform to the environmental regu-
lations of the country of origin.

P01062

Contents

Introduction

Aims of the guide

The purpose of this Student Text Guide to Michael Frayn's best-selling novel *Spies* is to enable you to organise your thoughts and responses to the novel, to deepen your understanding of key features and aspects, and to help you to address the particular requirements of examination questions in order to obtain the best possible grade. It will also prove useful to those writing a coursework piece on the novel by providing summaries, lists, analyses and references to help with the content and construction of the assignment.

It is assumed that you have already read and studied the novel under the guidance of a teacher or lecturer. This is a revision guide, not an introduction, although some of its content serves the purpose of providing initial background. It can be read in its entirety, or it can be used as a reference guide to specific and separate aspects of the novel.

The remainder of this Introduction consists of the Assessment Objectives, which summarise the requirements of the various exam boards and their schemes of assessment; revision advice, which gives a suggested programme for using the material in the guide; and guidance on writing examination essays.

The Text Guidance section consists of a series of subsections that examine key aspects of the book, including contexts, chapter summaries and notes, characters, themes and language. Emboldened terms within this section are glossed in the 'Literary terms and concepts' section on pp. 70–71.

The final section, Questions and Answers, gives extensive practical advice on writing essay answers of various types, along with mark schemes, model essay plans and some examples of marked work.

Page references are to the Faber and Faber paperback edition (2003, hardback 2002).

Assessment Objectives

The Assessment Objectives (AOs) for A-level English Literature are common to all boards:

AO1	communicate clearly the knowledge, understanding and insight appropriate to literary study, using appropriate terminology and accurate and coherent written expression
AO2i	respond with knowledge and understanding to literary texts of different types and periods

AO2ii	respond with knowledge and understanding to literary texts of different types and periods, exploring and commenting on relationships and comparisons between literary texts
AO3	show detailed understanding of the ways in which writers' choices of form, structure and language shape meanings
AO4	articulate independent opinions and judgements, informed by different interpretations of literary texts by other readers
AO5i	show understanding of the contexts in which literary texts are written and understood
AO5ii	evaluate the significance of cultural, historical and other contextual influences on literary texts and study

A summary of each Assessment Objective is given below and would be worth memorising:

AO1	clarity of written communication
AO2	informed personal response in relation to time and genre (literary context)
AO3	the creative literary process (context of writing)
AO4	critical and interpretative response (context of reading)
AO5	evaluation of influences (cultural context)

Assessment weighting

It is essential that you pay close attention to the Assessment Objectives, and their weighting, for the board for which you are entered. These are what the examiner will be looking for, and you must address them *directly* and *specifically*, in addition to proving general familiarity with and understanding of the text, and being able to present an argument clearly, relevantly and convincingly.

Remember, the examiners are seeking above all else evidence of an *informed personal response* to the text. A revision guide such as this can help you to understand the text and to form your own opinions, but it cannot replace your own ideas and responses as an individual reader.

Revision advice

For the examined units it is possible that either brief or extensive revision will be necessary because the original study of the text took place some time previously. It is therefore useful to know how to approach revision and which tried and tested methods

are considered the most successful for literature exams at all levels, from GCSE to degree finals. Below is a guide on how not to do it — think of reasons why not in each case.

Don't:

- leave it until the last minute
- assume you remember the text well enough and don't need to revise at all
- spend hours designing a beautiful revision schedule
- revise more than one text at the same time
- think you don't need to revise because it is an open-book exam
- decide in advance what you think the questions will be and revise only for those
- try to memorise particular essay plans
- reread texts randomly and aimlessly
- revise for longer than 2 hours in one sitting
- miss school lessons in order to work alone at home
- try to learn a whole ring-binder's worth of work
- tell yourself that character and plot revision is enough
- imagine that watching the video again is the best way to revise
- rely on a study guide instead of the text

There are no short cuts to effective exam revision; the only way to know a text well, and to know your way around it in an exam, is to have done the necessary studying. If you use the following six-stage method you will not only manage to revisit and reassess all previous work on the text but be able to distil, organise and retain your knowledge.

(1) Between a month and a fortnight before the exam, depending on your schedule, i.e. a simple list of stages with dates, you will need to read the text again, this time taking stock of all the underlinings and marginal annotations as well. As you read, collect onto sheets of A4 the essential ideas and quotations as you come across them. The acts of selecting key material and recording it as notes are natural ways of stimulating thought and aiding memory.

(2) Reread the highlighted areas and marginal annotations in your critical extracts and background handouts, and add anything useful from them to your list of notes and quotations. Then read your previous essays and the teacher's comments again. As you look back through essays written earlier in the course you should have the pleasant sensation of realising that you are now able to write much better on the text than you could before. You will also discover that much of your huge file of notes is redundant or repeated, and that you have changed your mind about some beliefs, so the distillation process is not too daunting. Selecting what is important is the way to crystallise your knowledge and understanding.

(3) During the run-up to the exam you need to have lots of essay plans to help you identify any gaps in your knowledge and give you practice in planning in 5–8 minutes. Past paper titles for you to plan are provided in this guide, some of which can be done as full timed essays — and marked strictly according to exam criteria — which will show whether length and timing are problematic for you. If you have not seen a copy of a real exam paper before you take your first module, ask to see a past paper so that you are familiar with the layout and rubric. For each text you are studying for the examination you need to know exactly which Assessment Objectives are being tested and where the heaviest weighting falls, as well as whether it is a closed or open-book exam. It would also be helpful if your teacher shared with you the examiners' reports on past papers.

(4) About a week before the exam, reduce your two or three sides of A4 notes to the size of a double-sided postcard of very small, dense writing. Collect a group of keywords by once again selecting and condensing, using abbreviations for quotations (first and last word) and character and place names (initials). Choosing and writing out the short quotations will help you to focus on the essential issues, and to recall them quickly in the exam. Make sure that your selection covers the main themes and includes examples of imagery, language, style, comments on character, examples of irony and other significant aspects of the text. Previous class discussion and essay writing will have indicated which quotations are useful for almost any essay title; select those that can serve more than one purpose. In this way a minimum number of quotations can have maximum application.

(5) You now have in a compact, accessible form all the material for any possible essay title. There are only half a dozen themes relevant to a literary text — although you should be aware that they may be expressed in a variety of ways — so if you have covered these you should not meet with any unpleasant surprises when you read the exam questions. You do not need to refer to your file of paperwork again, or even to the text. For the few days before the exam you can read through your handy postcard notes whenever and wherever you get the opportunity. Each time you read them, which should only take a few minutes, you are reminding yourself of all the information you will be able to recall in the exam to adapt to the general title or to support an analysis of particular passages.

(6) A fresh, active mind works wonders, and information needs time to settle, so don't try to cram just before the exam. Get a good night's sleep the night before so that you will be able to enter the exam room feeling the confidence of the well-prepared but relaxed candidate.

Writing examination essays

Essay content

One of the key skills you are being asked to demonstrate at A-level is the ability to select and tailor your knowledge of the text and its background to the question set in the exam paper. In order to reach the highest levels, you need to avoid 'pre-packaged' essays that lack focus, relevance and coherence, and that simply contain everything you know about the text. Be ruthless in rejecting irrelevant material, after considering whether it can be made relevant by a change of emphasis. Aim to cover the whole question, not just part of it; your response needs to demonstrate breadth and depth, covering the full range of text elements: character, event, theme and language. Essay questions are likely to refer to the key themes of the text, and therefore preparation of the text should involve extensive discussion and practice at manipulating these core themes. An apparently new angle is more likely to be something familiar presented in an unfamiliar way and you should not panic or reject the choice of question because you think you know nothing about it.

Read essay questions twice — the focus is not always immediately obvious. Many of them are several lines long, with several parts or sentences, some of which may be quotations from critics or from the text. You need to be sure of what a title means, and the assumptions behind it, before deciding whether to reject or attempt it.

Different views

Exam titles are open-ended in the sense that there is no obvious right answer, and you would therefore be unwise to give a dismissive, extreme or entirely one-sided response; the question would not have been set if the answer were not debatable. An ability and willingness to see both sides is an Assessment Objective and shows independence of judgement as a reader. Don't be afraid to explore the issues and avoid trying to tie the text into one neat interpretation. If there is ambiguity it is likely to be deliberate on the part of the author and must be discussed; literary texts are complex and often paradoxical, and it would be a misreading of them to suggest that there is only one possible interpretation. You are not expected, however, to argue equally strongly or extensively for both sides of an argument, since personal opinion is an important factor. It is advisable to deal with the alternative view at the beginning of your response, and then construct your own view as the main part of the essay. This makes it less likely that you will appear to cancel out your own line of argument.

Although the essay question may ask you to base your answer on one passage, you should ensure that you also refer to other parts of the text. As long as you stay focused on your main selection of material and on the key words in the question, you will get credit for making brief comments on other supporting material, which could include reference to critical works, works by other authors, or other works by the same author, as well as links to elsewhere in the same text.

Levels of response

A text can be responded to on four levels, but only the fourth one can receive the highest marks.

If you just give a character sketch or account of an incident this is the lowest and purely *descriptive* level, giving evidence of no skill other than being aware of the plot and characters; this does not even require a reading of the text itself. You are dealing only with the question 'What?' and in a limited context.

The next level, at about grade D, is a wider or more detailed *commentary* on events or characters, even making connections between them; but it still does not show real understanding of the text or an ability to interpret its themes.

For a C or low B grade you need to link different areas of the text, enter into *discussion* and explore major issues, though they may be in isolation from each other. This type of response addresses the question 'Why?'

A high B or A grade requires you to perform at an *analytical* level, showing an ability to think conceptually and to range across the whole text. You need to infer and draw conclusions based on an overview gained through a grasp of the overall themes that provide the coherent framework for the text. As well as character, plot and theme analysis, you will need to discuss language, style and structural elements, and link everything together. The question 'How?' is fully addressed at this level.

Length and timing

You will probably know by now whether length or timing is a problem for you. Although quality matters more than quantity, it is unlikely that you will have been able to fully explore and give a comprehensive answer to the question in fewer than three sides of A4 writing. You will typically have only 1 hour — minus planning and checking time — to write your essay, so you must practise the planning and writing stages under timed conditions until you are confident that you can give a full answer, ideally four sides, within the time limit. Finishing too early is not desirable, since the essay is unlikely to be as good as it could have been if the time had been fully utilised. The secret of length/timing success is to have developed a concise style and a brisk pace so that a lot of material is covered in a short space.

Choosing the right question

If there is a choice, the first skill you must show when presented with the exam paper is the ability to select the questions on your text that are best for you. This is not to say you should always go for the same type of essay, and if the question is not one with which you feel happy for any reason, you should consider the alternative, even if it is not a type you normally prefer. It is unlikely, but possible, that a question will contain a word you are not familiar with, in which case it would be safer to choose the other option.

Don't be tempted to choose a question because of its similarity to one you have already answered. Thinking on the spot usually produces a better result than attempting to recall a previous essay, which may have received only a mediocre mark in the first place. The exam question is unlikely to have exactly the same focus and your response may seem 'off centre' as a result, as well as stale and perfunctory in expression.

Underlining key words

When you have chosen your question, underline the key words in the title. There may be only one or as many as five or six, and it is essential that you discover how many aspects your response has to cover and fix in your mind the focus the answer must have. An essay that answers only half of the question cannot score top marks, however well that half is executed, and you need to demonstrate your responsiveness to all of the implications of the question. The key words often provide the sub-headings for planning and can suggest the overall approach to the essay.

Planning and structuring

To be convincing, your essay must demonstrate a logical order of thought and a sense of progression towards a conclusion. If you reproduce your ideas in random order as they occur to you, they are unlikely to form a coherent whole. Jumping between unrelated ideas is confusing for the reader and weakens the argument. If you find yourself repeating a quotation or writing 'as I said earlier' or 'as will be discussed later', you have probably not structured your essay effectively. There is no right structure for an essay, as long as there is one.

When planning an essay — which you can afford to spend 7–8 minutes on — your first action should be to brainstorm all the appropriate ideas and material you can think of, making a list in note form and using abbreviations to save time. You should aim for 10–12 separate points — about half a page — which will become the 10 or 12 paragraphs of your essay. If after a few minutes you do not have enough material, quickly switch to the other essay title. Beside each point, in a parallel column, indicate how you will support it. Next, group together the ideas that seem to belong together, and sort them into a logical order, using numbers. Identify which point will be the basis of your conclusion — the one with the overview — and move it to the end. The first points will follow from the essay title and definition of key words, and will be a springboard for your line of argument.

Remember that characters, events and aspects of language exist as vehicles for a text's themes — the real reason why texts are written. You need to become accustomed to planning by theme, using the other three elements to provide support and examples. Material relating to social and historical context needs to be integrated into your response and not just tacked on to the beginning or end.

Your plan should be cancelled with one diagonal line when you have finished writing your essay. The examiner does not want to start reading it by mistake, but will note that it exists, and it will raise expectations of a good essay. Your plan can be flexible — you can add extra material or decide to delete some during the writing stage — but it provides your basic structure and safety net.

Evidence

When selecting a point, check that you can support it adequately and convincingly; if not, substitute a better point. Unsupported assertion does not get much credit in exam essays and gives the impression of desperation or lack of familiarity with the text. Using about three paragraphs to a page, you should structure each paragraph by making a point and then supporting it with textual evidence, and a brief analysis of what it contributes to the overall answer to the question; without proof, paragraphs will be undeveloped and insubstantial.

Support for your argument can take three forms: reference, example or quotation. Aim for a mixture of these forms, as well as of different kinds of evidence (character, plot, image etc.). Quotation is not a substitute for thought or argument; it should support your interpretation and relate directly to the point you are making. It is the most effective way of proving familiarity and confidence in the use of the text, and of validating your claims.

When using other people's ideas as support, you must give credit where it is due, rather than trying to pass them off as your own. It is much more scholarly to attribute the reference, unless it is something which has been completely absorbed into your own interpretation and expressed in your own words. Otherwise, you can acknowledge source material by paraphrasing or summarising it, or by quoting exactly in inverted commas, mentioning the author in each case. A third option, if you have a quotation or idea you want to include but can't remember exactly where it came from, is to say 'as has been claimed by a critic' or 'it has been pointed out that …'.

Choose exactly the right quotation for what you are trying to prove, and use only the words that are appropriate. You can show that you have removed words from a quotation by using the ellipsis symbol (…) to replace the missing section. The cardinal rule is to quote accurately. If in doubt, it is safer to paraphrase than to guess wrongly.

Don't be afraid of using too much quotation; up to a quarter of an essay, or one per sentence, is acceptable. However, quotation for the sake of it, without interpretation or relevance, is useless, and you should aim for short integrated quotations of two or three words rather than longer ones, which take time and space.

Short quotations (less than one line of printed text) can be incorporated into your own sentence; longer quotations need to be introduced by a colon, started on a new line, and inset from both margins. If you are considering using such a lengthy quotation, pause and ask yourself if it is all necessary.

If you can't think of the right quotation to prove a point, reconsider whether the point is valid or worth making, or use an example or illustration instead. Remember that a quotation may prove more than one point; rather than repeating it, which weakens its effect, use it as a 'sandwich' between the two ideas it illustrates, which gives the impression of clever planning and structuring.

When making quotations, you do not need to give page references. Never give references instead of the quotation.

Put quotations in inverted commas; underline or use inverted commas for the title of the text.

Openings

Openings are the first indication to the examiner of whether you are an excellent, a mediocre or a weak student; it will be difficult to correct that first impression. By the end of the first paragraph you will have revealed whether you have the ability to write relevantly, accurately and clearly. For the most part, the best way into a literature essay is to define the implications and complexities of the title, starting with the underlined key words, especially if they are abstract concepts with a variety of possible interpretations (such as 'successful' and 'true'). Next, the widest and broadest application of the terms to the text will produce a range of ideas that could themselves be the structural headings for the essay.

As well as indicating the scope and framework for the answer, the introduction should provide brief and relevant contextual information. This may refer to the genre, the setting, the themes or the characters. It should not, however, be any of the following: a full plot synopsis; a summary of the life and work of the author; a repeat of the question; a vague and unfocused comment on life in general; or a list of any kind. Only points directly relevant to the question can be credited, so get started on the analysis as soon as possible. An introduction does not need to be more than a sentence or short paragraph and should never be longer than half a page.

Writing

With a useful plan you can write continuously — without needing to stop and think what to say next — and with fluency and coherence. You will need to write quickly and legibly. Think about appropriate expression and accuracy, asking yourself always 'What exactly am I trying to say?' Try to sound engaged and enthusiastic in your response; examiners are human and are affected by tone as much as the reader is with a text. It is actually possible to enjoy writing an essay, even in exam conditions.

Learn and apply the mnemonic acronym ACRID (accurate, concise, relevant, interesting and detailed).

Each paragraph should follow logically from the one before, either to continue the argument or to change its direction. Adverbial paragraph links — such as 'Furthermore', 'However', 'On the other hand' — are vital pointers to the progression of the argument. Paragraphs are a necessary courtesy to the reader and an indicator of point/topic change; paragraphs that are too long or too short reveal repetitive expression and lack of structure, or undeveloped ideas and lack of support respectively.

Avoid tentative or dogmatic statements, which make you sound either vague and uncertain or pompous and arrogant. Don't overstate or become sensational or emotional; steer clear of cliché and 'waffle'. Use accepted literary conventions, such as discussing literature in the present tense, avoiding calling a reader 'he', and using the surnames only of authors. It is safer to stick to the text itself than speculate about the author's intentions or personal viewpoint. Examiners are not looking for evidence of what you know about the author; they want to see your response to the text, and how you can apply your analysis to the question.

Write in a suitably formal, objective and impersonal style, avoiding ambiguous, repetitive and vague phrases. The aim is always clarity of thought and expression. Use appropriate technical terms to show competence instead of using unnecessary words. It is important to use exactly the right word and not the rough approximation which first comes to mind. Remember that every word should work for you and don't waste time on 'filler' expressions (such as 'As far as the novel is concerned') and adverbial intensifiers (such as 'very' and 'indeed'). Say something once, explore it, prove it and move on; you can only get credit for a point once. You don't need to preface every point with 'I think that' or 'I believe', since the whole essay is supposed to consist of what you think and believe. Don't keep repeating the terms of the title; the whole essay is supposed to be linked to the title, so you don't need to keep saying so. It must always be clear, however, how your point relates to the title; it must not be left to the reader to guess or mind-read what you think the connection may be.

Don't speculate, hypothesise, exaggerate or ask questions — it's your job to answer them. Feelings are not a substitute for thought in an academic essay; 'I feel' is usually a prelude to some unsubstantiated 'gushing'. Don't patronise the author by praising him or her for being clever or achieving something, and avoid copying your teacher through your marginal notes. The examiner will quickly spot if the whole class is using the same phrases, and will then know it is not your own idea that is being expressed. To quote from examiners' comments, to achieve a grade A, candidates are required to 'show a freshness of personal response as opposed to mere repetition of someone else's critical opinions, however good'. Whether the examiner agrees with you or not is irrelevant; it's the quality of the argument that counts.

While you are writing, keep an eye on the clock and aim to finish 5 minutes before the end of the exam to give you checking time. If you find you are running short of time, telescope the argument but try to cover all your points; as an emergency measure, break into notes to show what you would have written. This is better than spending your last precious 5 minutes finishing a particular sentence and not indicating what would have come next if you hadn't miscalculated the time.

Endings

Many students have trouble with endings, which are as important as openings. They are what the whole essay has been working towards and what the examiner has in mind when deciding upon a final mark. An ending needs to be conclusive, impressive and climactic, and not give the impression that the student has run out of time, ideas or ink. An ineffective ending is often the result of poor planning. Just repeating a point already made or lamely ending with a summary of the essay is a weak way of finishing, and cannot earn any extra marks.

Once again there are techniques for constructing conclusions. You need to take a step back from the close focus of the essay and make a comment that pulls together everything you've been saying and ties it into the overall significance of the text. A quotation from within or outside the text, possibly by the author, can be effective and definitive. You can also refer back to the title, or your opening statement, so that there is a satisfying sense of circularity for the reader, giving the impression that there is no more to be said on this subject.

Checking

Writing fast always causes slips of the mind and pen; these missing letters and words, misnamings of characters and genre confusions, are indistinguishable from ignorance and therefore must be corrected before submission. In addition, unchecked work will give a negative impression of your standards as a literature student, and examiners can always tell when work has been left unchecked.

Allow 5 minutes for checking your essay. Having spent several months studying a text it is worth making sure that your only exam essay on it is as good as you can make it. A few minutes spent checking can make the difference of a grade. Don't be afraid to cross words or phrases out; neat writing and immaculate presentation are not skills being assessed, but 'accurate and coherent written expression' is. As long as it is done neatly with one line, and the replacement word is written above legibly, correction counts in your favour rather than against you. Insert an asterisk in the text and put a longer addition at the bottom of the essay rather than trying to cram it into the margin, where it will be difficult to read and is encroaching on examiner territory. If you have forgotten to change paragraphs often enough, put in markers (//) when checking to show where a paragraph indentation should be.

When you check, you are no longer the writer but the reader of the text you have created, and a stranger too. Can you follow its line of argument? Are the facts accurate? Does it hang together? Is the vocabulary explicit? Is everything supported? And most importantly, but sadly often true, does it actually answer the question (even if the answer is that there is no answer)? You also need to watch out for spelling, grammar and punctuation errors, as well as continuing until the last second to improve the content and the expression. Don't waste time counting words.

There is no such thing as a perfect or model essay; flawed essays can gain full marks. There is always something more that could have been said, and examiners realise that students have limitations when writing under pressure in timed conditions. You are not penalised for what you didn't say in comparison to some idealised concept of the perfect answer, but are rewarded for the knowledge and understanding you have shown. It is not as difficult as you may think to do well, provided that you know the text in detail and have sufficient essay-writing experience. Follow the process of **choose**, **underline**, **select**, **support**, **structure**, **write** and **check**, and you can't go far wrong.

Text Guidance

Contexts

Biographical context

Michael Frayn was born on 8 September 1933 in Mill Hill in north London. His father, Tommy, was a deaf asbestos salesman, and his mother, Violet, a talented violinist, gave up her career to work as a shop assistant. The family moved two years later to Ewell in Surrey, the setting for *Spies*, where Frayn grew up and attended a small private preparatory school. His mother died just at the end of the Second World War when he was 12 years old. His father was no longer able to afford private school fees, and Frayn was sent to Kingston Grammar School. He later commented:

> I shared all the suburban prejudices about public education and assumed I was going to a rough school. In fact the private school had been all beating and bullying, and Kingston Grammar was perfectly regulated; it took a long time for my suspicions to settle, but it was my good fortune to be sent there because it gave me a good education.

> from an interview in the *Guardian*, 31 January 2002, available online at
> http://education.guardian.co.uk/higher/arts/story/0,9848,642291,00.html

After school Frayn was required to undertake National Service in the army, where he was taught Russian in order to do intelligence work. He subsequently went to Cambridge University where he studied Russian, French and Moral Sciences. He had always wanted to be a journalist, and found his first job as a reporter with the *Manchester Guardian*. He then began a parallel career as a writer, first as a novelist and then as a playwright.

He wrote nine novels prior to *Spies*, as well as 13 plays and numerous translations, screenplays and collections of journalistic articles. Although he initially wrote humorous works, he has tackled more serious topics during the last ten years or so, although humour remains an element in his work. He has shown a consistent interest in the historical context of his works, and his play *Copenhagen* (1998), about the ethical dilemmas facing scientists involved in German attempts to develop atomic weapons during the Second World War, examines in detail themes of loyalty and betrayal in wartime (an interesting counterpart, although on a very different scale, to *Spies*). He has also displayed an interest in German history and culture; both *Copenhagen* and his most recent play, *Democracy*, are set in Germany, and it could be argued that although *Spies* is set in England, Stephen spends as much of his life in Germany as he does in Surrey.

In an interview published in the *Daily Mail* on 2 December 2004, Frayn threw intriguing light on the genesis of *Spies*:

> I'd been trying to write the book for 20 years. Then I remembered a
> friend who was the leader in all our games; the one with the imagination.

He laid down whether we could play cowboys or policemen. He was always the chief character.

One day he said to me, out of the blue, 'My mother is a German spy', and I understood that this was the start of a new game, in which we would follow his mother around and wear false beards. We did trail her for a couple of hours, but when she didn't steal the plans for a new aircraft, or send any radio messages to the Germans, we got bored and gave up. Many years later, I started to wonder what would have happened if we had followed her for a longer period — what secrets we might have discovered. After that point, the book is pure fiction.

Source: www.dailymail.co.uk/pages/live/articles/books/authors.html?
in_page_id=1826&in_article_id=328573

Frayn has received numerous awards and prizes for his work. His novel *Headlong* was short-listed for the Booker Prize for Fiction in 1999, and *Spies* won the Whitbread Novel Award in 2002. The play *Copenhagen* won several prizes for drama.

Michael Frayn is married to the biographer and critic Claire Tomalin. He was formerly married to Gillian Palmer, with whom he has three children.

Historical context: the Second World War

The Second World War was the most destructive war in human history. During its course of nearly six years (1939–45), more than 55 million people perished, many times exceeding the horrors of the First World War (1914–18). Yet, for all that, attitudes to the Second World War remain curiously mixed. There has been an outpouring in recent years of popular historical works on the war, which have topped bestseller lists, a trend that shows no sign of abating; there has also been a resurgence of novels set during the conflict, of which *Spies* is but one example. Why is this?

There are many possible answers to this question, and sociologists and cultural historians will no doubt debate them for years to come. Some relate to the unique nature of the conflict itself, involving as it did civilian populations in all the European combatant countries for a period of years, and to the consequences of this experience for social cohesion and in the collective memory. Others relate to the uniquely clear moral dimension of the conflict: this was a war for principles, values and morality. The enemy was uniquely evil, and the confirmation of this with the exposure of the extermination camps in the closing days of the war cemented this idea in the popular imagination. Others again relate to the extraordinarily ambivalent attitudes held by many people, then and now, towards the whole phenomenon of Nazi Germany. Many recent historical studies now feel able to admit openly what has been unspoken for 60 years: the Wehrmacht (the German armed forces) was the outstanding military organisation of the war, out-performing every other participant to an unprecedented

degree. Its most notorious arm, the Waffen SS (the military corps of the Nazi party), attracts adulation and revulsion in millions of people. It is no coincidence that the market for Wehrmacht memorabilia, and even more so for SS items, shows exceptional vitality, although a proportion of this interest is related to modern neo-Nazi political movements such as the National Front.

A further set of reasons for the current interest in the Second World War relates to the nature of the fighting: whereas the trench warfare of the First World War allowed no opening for tactical innovation or even, in any conventional sense, for heroism, the highly mobile warfare of the Second World War allowed brilliant generalship to be displayed (almost exclusively by the Germans) and led to tactical and strategic innovation on a huge scale. Battlefield casualties were low by the standards of the previous war, except on the Eastern Front (in the war between Germany and the Soviet Union); Britain, for example, lost 326,000 men in combat, compared with 703,000 killed (and more than 1.6 million wounded) in the Great War. Those who fought in the war had a sense of purpose, and of the value of their contribution, which was not present in the First World War.

The background to the war has three aspects: first, the treatment that Germany received at the end of the First World War left the Germans deeply bitter and determined to overthrow the hated Versailles Treaty. Second, the Wall Street Crash in the USA in 1929 did severe damage to the economies of all the countries of Europe. The resulting social unrest threatened the fabric of societies throughout the continent and led to extreme, anti-democratic parties receiving wide support; the Nazi party in Germany came to power in the wake of the economic crisis. Third and most fundamentally, the war was about competing political ideologies. By the 1930s, there were three utterly irreconcilable sets of ideas in western Europe about how societies should be organised, and how wealth and influence should be distributed.

- **Democracy:** the belief that all citizens should participate in choosing a government, and that all citizens should enjoy equal rights. This dominant philosophy was greatly weakened in the 1930s by the failure of democratic governments to deal with the consequences of the Wall Street Crash.
- **Communism:** this idealistic philosophy, created by Karl Marx and Friedrich Engels in their *Communist Manifesto* of 1848, had become a powerful alternative since the success of the Bolshevik revolution in Russia in 1917.
- **Fascism/Nazism:** anti-democratic movements, which were extremely nationalistic, seeking to unite a nation rather than divide it as democracy was thought to do. The individual was to be subordinated to the needs of the state; and in the Nazi version, was to play a role in the striving of mankind towards its destiny. The Nazi philosophy also included a vicious and spurious racism, which believed that the Germans were members of an Aryan master race; all other races were viewed as inferior and, in the case of the Jews, sub-human.

The war commenced in September 1939 with the Nazi invasion of Poland. Britain sent a large part of its army to France as the British Expeditionary Force (BEF) in the autumn of 1939 to reinforce the French and to await the inevitable attack, which came in May 1940. The German tactic of Blitzkrieg (highly mobile warfare spearheaded by tanks) took the French by surprise. They were hampered by weak and divided leadership, and the Germans broke through immediately. The BEF made a fighting withdrawal to the port of Dunkirk, from where a large number of troops (more than 300,000) were successfully evacuated to Britain. France fell and came under German occupation, but in the ensuing Battle of Britain the fighters of the Royal Air Force held off the German Luftwaffe (air force). The planned German invasion of Britain was abandoned in September.

Thereafter, the British engaged the Germans in the deserts of North Africa, but until the Allied invasion of Normandy in June 1944 (D-Day) and the final push into Germany, the British could only attack Germany itself by air. The role of the RAF's Bomber Command was central: waves of bombers flew to Germany nightly, to bomb the cities and factories in the hope of breaking German civilian morale and damaging the productive capacity of German industry. Casualties among bomber aircrew were high, and the ever-present risk of being shot down over Germany meant either death or captivity as a prisoner of war.

The German invasion of the Soviet Union in June 1941 proved the turning point of the war, for Hitler had met his match in the leader of the Soviet Union, Stalin, and after nearly four years of often bestial fighting with huge casualties, the Russian Red Army struck into Berlin in late April 1945 and destroyed both Nazism and Germany.

In parallel with the war in Europe, a war in Asia developed following the unprovoked Japanese attack on the US fleet at Pearl Harbor in Hawaii in December 1941. This led to US involvement in the European theatre of war (the US Air Force made a major contribution to the bombing of Germany, and contributed the largest forces to D-Day and the subsequent campaign in western Europe). The war in Asia ended with the dropping of atomic bombs on the Japanese cities of Hiroshima and Nagasaki in August 1945.

The British army in the Second World War

It may be helpful for the reader to understand the structure and ranks of the army at the time. The British army has always maintained a fundamental distinction between officers and 'other ranks'. Officers took the 'King's commission' and swore an oath of personal loyalty to the monarch. They were required to be gentlemen, and were bound by a strict code of conduct. They were therefore, in practice, invariably from the upper or middle classes. Aristocrats generally took commissions in the Guards or the Household Cavalry; middle-class officers led all the other regiments and units. The 'other ranks' were, in peacetime, recruited entirely from

the working class. Although subject to a strict disciplinary code, they did not take a commission (indeed, senior 'other ranks' were known as 'non-commissioned officers' or NCOs). NCOs wore their badge of rank on the sleeves of their tunics; officers wore them on their epaulettes.

The Second World War: the home front

The Second World War was a 'total war' in a way that the Great War had not been. The development of medium-range bombers meant that all of Britain was within range of the Luftwaffe, operating from airfields in France and the Low Countries. Aerial bombing was viewed as a wonder weapon, which could destroy a country's ability to wage war as well as causing a political crisis by destroying the morale of the civilian population. The Blitz — the indiscriminate bombing of London by the Luftwaffe from the summer of 1940 onwards — became a powerful part of the myth of British fortitude during the war. The population of London experienced almost nightly bombing during extended periods of the war, and civilian casualties were high.

The experience of night-time raids and waiting fearfully in air-raid shelters (either communal, or the Anderson shelters built in back gardens) for the all-clear to sound meant, at the very least, disturbed sleep patterns, not to mention the continuous climate of fear. Air-raid wardens watched for any breach of the blackout, which was designed to make the job of the enemy bombers harder but which became a daily irritation, especially as some wardens pursued their duties officiously. Many civilians played their part as wardens or fire watchers, or in the fire service. The fear of a gas attack (as in the trenches during the First World War) led to the issue of gas masks to all civilians, and during the early years children were required to carry them everywhere in case of a surprise attack. People lived by the air-raid sirens — the wailing, which warned of a raid, and the continuous all-clear, which meant that the threat was over for a while.

Total war made itself felt in other areas as well. The entire economy was mobilised for the war effort and was subject to tight central control. Virtually all commodities were rationed; petrol was effectively unobtainable for private use. The labour market came under government control, and those young men who were not conscripted into the armed forces were required to do 'war-work', as were a large number of women. The great majority of men aged between 18 and 41 served in the army, navy or air force. While many volunteered on the outbreak of war, those who were conscripted were initially enlisted as 'other ranks', whatever their background, with subsequent opportunities for appropriate candidates to become officers. This meant that the rigid class structure of the British forces was undermined for the duration of the war, as many men who at any other time would have become officers served in the ranks.

Many children were evacuated from the larger cities, especially London, and were billeted with unrelated families in safer country districts, leading in many cases to tension. Some were sent overseas to Canada and elsewhere for the duration of the war, and there were tragic cases of evacuee ships being torpedoed and sunk en route to their supposedly safer destinations.

Spies and the Second World War

Although *Spies* is set during the Second World War, and the war supplies key components of the plot (the search for a German spy in the Close would not have the same urgency in a time of peace), it nevertheless shows very little sign of people being affected by the war. Frayn does not explicitly state the location, but there are enough clues to suggest that it is set in a recently developed suburb of London. Frayn lived in Ewell in Surrey during the war and it is reasonable to assume that the setting is substantially autobiographical. This area was under some of the main routes used by Luftwaffe bombers on their way to London, but apart from the 'stray German incendiary bomb' (p. 30) that destroyed Miss Durrant's house, there is very little reference to this. The cupboard under the stairs had been used as a shelter (why do none of the houses appear to have an Anderson shelter in the garden?), but only in Chapter 8 is reference made to the Battle of Britain ('an earlier summer') and sirens and searchlights. People do not seem to be affected significantly by rationing, and the boys go to school as normal. If they were evacuated earlier, there is no mention of it.

The precise date is not given, but there are good reasons for supposing that it may be quite late in the war: German bombing attacks are now rare, the Battle of Britain and the Blitz are distant memories, and Uncle Peter is bombing eastern German cities such as Chemnitz, Leipzig and Zwickau. These cities were not in fact systematically bombed until January 1945, a mere four months from the end of the war, at which point the outcome was clear and the threat of German spying negligible. This would not, of course, have been apparent to two young boys. However, given that the events clearly span the course of a summer, and given that Germany surrendered in May 1945, the novel cannot be set later than the summer of 1944. So is the wartime setting important at all? Yes, both because it gives the cause of Uncle Peter's breakdown, and requires him to hide as a fugitive.

The RAF bomber campaign against Germany

Once the threat of invasion ended in 1940, the focus of war moved elsewhere. The Royal Air Force's Bomber Command began to bomb Germany as early as 1940, but it was not until the arrival of heavy four-engined bombers such as the Lancaster and Halifax from early 1942 that they began to have any significant effect. Arthur 'Bomber' Harris became the commander at the same time and began the practice of 'area bombing', in which whole German cities were designated as targets. By the summer of 1942 'thousand-bomber raids' were being launched

against industrial cities in the western part of Germany. Following the Allied invasion of Europe on D-Day, the raids became even more intensive and the attention of the bombers moved steadily eastwards, to cities such as Chemnitz, Leipzig and Zwickau.

The bomber raids against Germany were intensely dangerous. It took several hours for the large, slow-moving bombers to reach their targets (longer for targets in eastern Germany). Although the RAF invariably flew at night, there were anti-aircraft guns in huge numbers, guided by searchlights and radar, and substantial numbers of night fighters to contend with. During the course of the war, some 55,000 Bomber Command aircrew were killed on missions. Half of all aircrew were lost during their first ten missions; less than one in eight crews survived a 'tour' of 50 missions. Many aircrew found the prolonged stress of their missions intolerable.

Although the policy of area bombing was a mirror of the Luftwaffe's Blitz on London, which introduced the idea of bombing civilian populations to break their morale, it was morally controversial even at the time. It is because of such a raid that the privet hedge of Braemar is available to the boys as a hideout, its owner having been killed by a Luftwaffe bomb. We are reminded that this is what Uncle Peter and his colleagues were doing by the information, given in the final chapter, that Stephen's innocent (and presumably Jewish) aunt and her children were killed by an Allied bombing raid during the war.

Literary context

The Second World War novel

Spies is one of a very large number of novels set in, or including, the Second World War. 'Historical' novels have always been popular, but in many cases the historical setting has merely lent colour to an otherwise unremarkable story (you could argue this of *Spies*). The particular attraction of the Second World War as a context for contemporary novelists, apart from the fact that many of them lived through it, is the extraordinarily rich range of experiences it offered. No other conflict, arguably no other period in history, impacted upon the lives of so many people in such a memorable or devastating way. It was 'total war' as no previous war had been, in the sense that civilian populations were directly targeted for indiscriminate bombing and were profoundly affected in a range of ways including rationing, evacuation and conscription for military or civilian service.

Significant novels about the Second World War began to be published soon after it ended. A model that became increasingly common was for the war to act as the culmination of a story that started during the interwar years. This allowed the novelist to show how characters were changed by the experiences of war, which typically heightened feelings and reactions and frequently involved tragedy. In novels set in peacetime, the death of younger characters can generally only be secured by crime or freak accident, whereas in the Second World War death was so common, from such a range of causes, that it can become a convenient plot device.

Evelyn Waugh's *Brideshead Revisited*, published as early as 1945, allows the reader to see how its spoilt characters respond to the hardships of war. The war section in Anthony Powell's great novelistic sequence *A Dance to the Music of Time* (1951–75) has the same effect. Evelyn Waugh's magisterial *Sword of Honour* trilogy (1952–61) is entirely set during the war, as are Olivia Manning's Balkan and Levant trilogies (1960–80). More recently, many novelists have set works in this period; for example, Louis de Bernières's *Captain Corelli's Mandolin* (1994) explores the conflict of loyalties that develops when a member of an occupying army becomes emotionally involved with a local woman; Sebastian Faulks's *Charlotte Gray* (1999) examines the role of British agents sent into occupied France.

While some Second World War novels have concerned themselves directly with combatants and combat, others have focused on civilians and how the war affected them. Helen Dunmore's *The Siege* (2001), for example, examines the fate of Russian civilians during the epic siege of Leningrad from 1941 to 1944.

The Second World War changed British society in a number of ways, which novelists have observed and recorded. Life in the 1930s was seen as carefree and, often, irresponsible; the advent of war, bringing rationing and shared suffering, caused everyone to 'pull together' for the common good. Gerald Durrell's *My Family and Other Animals* (1956), for example, records a peacetime idyll destroyed by the outbreak of war. There was also, during a war that lasted nearly six years, considerable paranoia about enemy spies. *Carrie's War* (1973) by Nina Bawden examines what it was like to be a child in wartime England, as does John Boorman's great film *Hope and Glory* (1987). In *The English Patient* (1992) by Michael Ondaatje, the innocent multinational team of geographers working to map Egypt's western desert is tragically broken apart by the forces of war.

The coming of age novel

The transition from childhood to adulthood, via the stressful interlude of adolescence, is a period that is engraved in the memories of most adults. It is during this time that life-changing experiences are undergone, and in many cases the character of the adult is determined by especially significant, traumatic or transcendent experiences. It has been a focus of attention for many writers, and there are innumerable novels, poems and plays explicitly addressing this absorbing and universal theme. *Spies* may be seen as a 'coming of age' novel because it is centrally concerned with a protagonist on the cusp of adolescence who finds himself in a situation which he cannot quite understand, and his immature responses have immediate and devastating consequences for the adults directly concerned. What equally interests Frayn, though, are the more subtle long-term consequences for the central child–adolescent as he comes to appreciate the

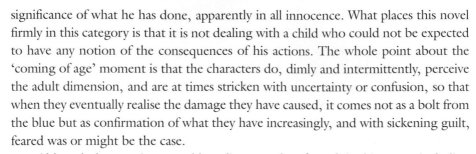

significance of what he has done, apparently in all innocence. What places this novel firmly in this category is that it is not dealing with a child who could not be expected to have any notion of the consequences of his actions. The whole point about the 'coming of age' moment is that the characters do, dimly and intermittently, perceive the adult dimension, and are at times stricken with uncertainty or confusion, so that when they eventually realise the damage they have caused, it comes not as a bolt from the blue but as confirmation of what they have increasingly, and with sickening guilt, feared was or might be the case.

Although there are innumerable earlier examples of novels in this **genre**, including Dickens's *Great Expectations*, perhaps the most obviously relevant is L. P. Hartley's *The Go-Between*, published in 1953 but set in the summer of the year 1900. It can be seen as the prototype of *Spies* in that the impressionable young character, probably turning from 12 to 13, is used as a lovers' go-between by adults who take advantage of the naivety of the child (and so, arguably, can be seen as receiving their just deserts for such manipulation), and also in that the momentous events occur during a memorable summer.

The latter seems to be a motif of special significance for British authors; because the British weather is so depressingly grey and wet for so much of the year, a brief and glorious summer often stands out in the memory as a uniquely blessed time. Seen nostalgically through rose-tinted vision, all the summers of one's childhood are remembered as sunnier than they actually were. For such a time to be associated with coming of age, rites of passage or some form of initiation into the adult world makes it especially resonant. It is also the only time of the year when children are free for an extended period of time, during the long summer holiday, and when the weather allows them to be out of the house. It is the end of the school year in Britain too, so the changes that occur in a long summer are reinforced by a new status on returning to school. There is also the comparison with nature: summer is the season of development and maturation, of coming into full blossom before autumn decay. Laurie Lee's *Cider With Rosie* (1959) is another example of a novel that enshrines this time of transition.

It is perhaps worth noting that the transition from child to adult has been marked by formal rituals, trials and celebrations in virtually all primitive civilisations throughout history (but without the 'adolescent' or 'teenager' stage, which is a postwar marketing invention; prior to this, children modelled themselves on adults in their beliefs, dress and lifestyle). It is arguable that it is the absence of such recognised structures in modern Western societies that renders the emerging adult peculiarly sensitive to life-changing events at this time. What is notable about *The Go-Between* is the author's clear indication that the events of that faraway summer have scarred the young Leo so permanently that he is unable to grow up into a fully independent adult, or to form adult relationships throughout the remainder of his life. Frayn's Stephen is not in such a hopeless situation;

nevertheless, the events of the wartime summer have damaged him sufficiently that he feels the need to travel back (as does the elderly Leo in *The Go-Between*) to the site of the horror in order to exorcise it.

Another important coming of age novel is James Joyce's *Portrait of the Artist as a Young Man* (1916), whose central character, Stephen Dedalus, may be the source of the name of Frayn's Stephen.

Postmodernism

'Modernism' is the term applied to the literary (and artistic) movements of the first half of the twentieth century. Modernist literature typically experiments with form, depends on symbol and myth as structural principles, and explores the workings of the unconscious mind as a result of the influence of Freudian analysis. The 'stream of consciousness' mode was invented to capture the flux and development within the individual thought process and to convey the complexity and instability of personality. Modernist texts looked back to mythology for parallels for the individual beleaguered by social expectations and threatened by the ending of an era; the *Odyssey* motif (as in James Joyce's *Ulysses)* was thought particularly appropriate to represent the difficult and changing journey of life.

'**Postmodernism**', which succeeded it in the later twentieth century, shares the preoccupations of Modernism but goes further in that it mocks and rejects traditional linear narrative, and refuses to give the reader the comfort of **closure**. Central to Postmodernist writing is the author's aim of unsettling and **deconstructing** accepted notions about language, identity, and about writing itself. It tends to cross the dividing line between high and popular culture, and it exposes and discredits previously accepted attitudes to female, colonial, religious and political oppression. It is **self-reflexive** in calling attention to the way it has come into existence and to its own nature as something that has been deliberately constructed. As a consequence, it makes us reflect on writing in general and on the triple relationship between author, character and reader. Questions of identity in Postmodernist fiction are created by *parallelism, binary oppositions, doublings,* mixing fictional and historical characters, twisting well-known myths, and drawing attention to the artificiality of all representation.

Postmodernism is based on the premise that language is ultimately an unstable and unreliable medium of communication, while still using language ironically to tell us so (as summed up in the conundrum of whether we can believe the Cretan who says 'All Cretans are liars'). It proves the impossibility of reducing a text to a single truth, in order to cast doubt on the possibility of defining such concepts as history. Borrowings from earlier texts set up echoes and also show us the blind spots of these earlier texts. Postmodernist writing is therefore built on ambivalence and is fundamentally paradoxical. It asserts and then subversively undermines such abstract principles as value, order, meaning, control, certainty,

morality — in the process undermining itself and any tendency to consistency or a single interpretation.

Because large-scale historical interpretations, such as Marxism, have enslaved large parts of the world in the past by being absolute and universal, the Postmodernist writer suggests that small-scale, modest, local narratives are needed to replace them and to restore humanity. We need provisional, little stories that are strong enough to guide us but make no claims beyond the here and now.

It is possible to convey story and history in other ways than the standard narration technique of omniscient narrator in the past tense with interludes of character dialogue. A Postmodernist text is a collage which reveals that there are many ways of seeing, depending on who you are, where you are looking from, and what your social and historical experience is.

The main issues to be aware of when dealing with contemporary texts and Postmodernist critical theory are:

- **Plurality**: because texts can be read in different ways by different readers at different times and in different contexts, there is never a single meaning or a single 'right answer' that can be taught and learned. Readers must learn how to reach their own conclusions about texts and writers, taking account of other interpretations in the process.
- **Intertextuality**: writers do not write, nor do readers read, in a literary vacuum. The relationships between texts, and the comparisons that can be drawn between them, illuminate the writing and reading. This is why it is now a requirement for all A-level English Literature specifications to contain comparative study of whole texts.
- **Contextuality**: again, writers write and readers read within a number of contexts: social, cultural and historical. These affect the ways in which texts can be read. Candidates at AS must show their awareness of these influences, while at A2 they should be able to evaluate the significance of contexts for the way in which texts are read.

Spies clearly falls within the definition of Postmodernist texts because the author refuses to write a conventional narrative (see 'Language, style, structure and voice' on pp. 65–70 of this guide).

Chapter summaries and notes

Chapter 1 (pp. 3–6) — viewpoint: present day

This opening chapter is set in the present day and, although this does not become clear until the end of the book, in Germany, where Stephen now lives. The importance of nostalgia is immediately stated: 'The third week of June and there it is again' (p. 3). The narrator feels 'a restlessness' (p. 3) and states 'I know that the place I should like to be off to is my childhood' (p. 3). He has a daughter and grandchildren, and has arrived at that stage of life when people ask questions such as 'How many of the others are still alive? How many of them remember?' (p. 5). He resolves to go to London — 'that far-off nearby land' (pp. 3–4). Chapter 1 also introduces the shocking, remembered smell, of privet in June, which he associates (reminiscent of Marcel Proust) with the events of that momentous, far-off summer; 'it has a kind of sexual urgency to it' (p. 3) because it is associated with his first sexual awakening. His daughter describes it as 'Liguster', but the English name is privet.

Chapter 2 (pp. 9–33) — viewpoint: present day

The narrator returns to the Close, for the first time in 50 (or 60) years, and states 'Everything is as it was, I discover when I reach my destination, and everything has changed' (p. 9). This paradox lies at the heart of the novel, and he refers to it several times. He gives an account, in the present tense ('I stand on the corner') as he walks up the street, and imagines it as it was. This is the beginning of the process by which the present-day narrator conjures his former self, initially describing events as if he was an observer, then little by little merging with the younger boy. He describes a number of the houses, and 'follows' young Stephen to 'Chollerton', the house of his friend Keith. He interweaves the present and the past, thereby confusing the reader about the viewpoint of the narrative. The 'six random words' ('My mother…is a German spy'), the hook upon which the narrative is hung, are introduced (finally uttered on p. 33).

He first refers to Stephen Wheatley (which we later understand to be another distancing device, as old Stephen is now Stefan Weitzler) on p. 12, 'the awkward boy who lives in that unkempt house', and describes him as if he can see him, as an outside observer — a device he intermittently maintains throughout the book. He at times seems to be walking beside Stephen, but at other times he merges with him.

He introduces several other residents of the Close, before describing in detail Keith, Keith's parents, and Uncle Peter and Auntie Dee — the key characters. He also introduces his theme: 'It's so difficult to remember what order things occurred in — but if you can't remember *that*, then it's impossible to work out which led to which, and what the connection was' (p. 32). He also, rather blatantly, signposts the limitations of an account based on memory from so long ago, a device he repeats several times: 'No, wait. I've got that wrong' (p. 31).

References and allusions

p. 15, the Trossachs by Alfred Hollings RA. The Trossachs is a natural park area of Scotland; these were presumably typical sentimental paintings. Hollings is fictitious; 'RA' indicates that he is a member of the Royal Academy.

p. 16, preparatory school. A private school for boys aged from seven to 13; its role was to prepare them to take the Common Entrance examination (see below).

p. 16, Common Entrance. Introduced in 1904, these academic examinations were the selection mechanism for all prestigious private (or independent) schools (known in Britain as 'public schools').

p. 17, pipeclay his cricket boots. Pipeclay was a whitening cream used for sports equipment.

p. 18, superheterodyne. A form of high performance radio receiver.

p. 21, the Duration. The duration of the war. This became a form of shorthand for all the aspects of life, which had been put on hold for 'the duration' of the conflict.

p. 25, three famous initials. The Royal Air Force or RAF. Because of the role of the RAF in saving the country from invasion during the Battle of Britain, it was seen as especially heroic.

p. 29, saccharine. A more refined sweetener than the sugar used by Stephen's family; it also suggests Mrs Hayward's consciousness of her appearance (saccharine is less fattening than sugar).

p. 29, adjutant. In the army, a junior officer who carries out the instructions of a senior officer.

Chapter 3 (pp. 37–57) — viewpoint oscillates, immersed in the past

Stephen and Keith begin to observe and record Mrs Hayward's movements. She pretends to shoot them — 'as if we were children' (p. 41) — but also as if she knew what they were about to do. That afternoon while she sleeps upstairs they go through her desk in the lounge — and find the x's in her diary (one every 4 weeks, occasionally adjusted by a day or two) and the — very rare — exclamation marks (including one on her and Ted's wedding anniversary). The reader, of course, instantly recognises this simple code (the x's mark her periods, and the exclamation marks denote the rare occasions on which she has sex with her husband); the boys do not, and with false naivety the narrator does not comment.

She catches them; and they go into the privet hedge outside the ruins of 'Braemar' and set up their secret camp. Keith forces Stephen to swear a blood oath of secrecy. Keith writes the title 'PRIVET' (meaning 'private': an **irony**, of course, in the privet hedge, but Frayn does not point this out). Note that Keith, described as in every way superior, mis-spells many words; Stephen knows this but dare not point it out (compare the writing of 'LOGBOOK — SECRIT' on p. 40).

References and allusions

p. 41, two and fourpence. The currency of Britain in the 1940s was composed of pounds, shillings and pence; the current (decimal) system was introduced in 1971. Two shillings and four pence was quite a substantial sum at a time when the average weekly pocket money for a boy would have been about sixpence.

p. 45, as silently as Sioux. Boys at the time regularly read the *Boy's Own Paper* and other similar magazines, which typically included highly **stereotyped** adventure stories. The silent tracking skills of the Sioux 'Indians' (native Americans) was one such stereotype.

p. 46, books of tuppenny-halfpenny stamps. Colloquial term for stamps costing two and a half pence, the standard rate for a letter at the time; a 'book' of six could be purchased.

p. 48, Ted to OH dinner. This must refer to the annual dinner for the former students of his private school. There are several candidates; the most likely is Old Harrovians (Harrow School, a socially elite school in west London).

p. 55, the wafer and the wine. The bayonet is being likened to the sacrament in (Christian) Mass or Communion; Roman Catholics believe that the consecrated wafer both becomes the real body of Christ and, at the same time, remains a wafer.

Chapter 4 (pp. 61–82) — viewpoint: entirely in the past

A brief glimpse of Stephen being bullied at school; he is frustrated that he cannot get out to carry on observing Mrs Hayward, but his father is for once home and there is a rather painful conversation between them. Stephen speculates on 'Why my father has never killed any Germans' (p. 64) (note the **irony**, upon which the narrator again does not comment) and dismisses 'my unsatisfactory family' (p. 65). Frustrated during the week, the boys watch all Saturday morning. Stephen almost loses interest and breaks free from Keith — when Mrs Hayward appears. They follow her several times, and on two of them she impossibly disappears, and then reappears in Auntie Dee's house. The final time, she is wiping something slimy off her hands.

References and allusions

p. 63, cabbalistic. About secret knowledge. The Cabbala is (although most people do not appreciate this) an ancient Jewish system of mystical wisdom.

p. 64, a sheeny. A slang word for a Jew.

p. 67, secateurs. Pruning shears used by gardeners.

p. 67, the down line. By convention, all railway lines leading to London are known as the 'up line', and those leading away from London are the 'down line'. Because Ewell is south of London, the 'down line' is southbound.

p. 71, the 419 to school. The route number of the bus Stephen took to school each morning. The 400 series implies a green 'London Country' bus, evidence that they are in the outer suburbs of London.

p. 79, the double summer time. In Britain the clocks 'go forward' one hour in spring; this is sometimes known as 'daylight saving time'. During the Second World War the clocks went forward two hours.

p. 79, as academic as scot and lot. 'Scot and lot' was a phrase used to refer to medieval local taxes, so something of purely academic interest.

Chapter 5 (pp. 85–110) — viewpoint: present day initially, then past

The chapter starts in the present day: 'A surprising thought comes to this old man, as he looks at the district now from the perspective of the years' (p. 85). The narrator walks and comments — on the recency of the Close then, and of what has happened to the area since.

On p. 89 he reverts to the dramatic present tense and the viewpoint of the past. Stephen has worked out that Mrs Hayward turns right under the railway tunnel, not left to the shops, so they explore that way — in 'the Lanes'. It is like a boys' adventure story. They climb up onto the embankment, and see Mrs Hayward. Keith finds the metal trunk hidden in the undergrowth, with the cigarette packet and the piece of paper marked 'x'.

The next day, Stephen is visited in the hideout by Barbara Berrill (the first time) who 'reveals' that Auntie Dee has a 'boyfriend'.

Mrs Hayward comes over one evening and visits Stephen in the hide in the hedge. 'That's what you're up to in here, is it? Keeping watch on us all, and writing it all down in your logbook?' (p. 107).

She gives a warning: 'For instance, I think it might be perhaps just a *tiny* bit rude if you actually followed people around' (p. 107). She continues: 'Keith's easily led, as I'm sure you realise' (p. 108). Stephen is incredulous. Then she enlists him: 'So you see I'm trusting you. I'm putting you on your honour' (p. 109). He shows a flash of empathy: 'I feel pained that she's had to humiliate herself before me in this way' (p. 110).

References and allusions

p. 85, a Potemkin village. Villages allegedly constructed by the Russian minister Grigori Potemkin to fool the Empress Catherine in the eighteenth century; therefore any village suddenly created just in time for people to come upon it.

Chapter 6 (pp. 113–33) — viewpoint: entirely in the past

Awakened by the full moon, Stephen determines to go through the tunnel at night, so he will not be disturbed. He goes to the chest to find what Mrs Hayward left there;

he feels cloth. Then he hears a man approach: the moon comes out, and the man sees him and runs away. Stephen, too, runs back home — and finds his parents in the street, looking for him. He is soaking (perhaps he has fallen into the puddle under the bridge) but he has in his hand a blue darned sock from the chest. He reveals nothing. He shows it to Keith (the juxtaposed reference to 'Uncle Peter's straightforward gaze from the mantelpiece' (p. 120) gives the reader a clue); they go under the bridge — and find the chest missing. Keith perceptively reconstructs Stephen's fear and panic, and Stephen is humiliated — Keith accurately describes him as 'like a little baby' (p. 124). Note that they are really both very young boys, although Keith despises Stephen for it: when someone passes, both bury their faces in the grass to avoid being seen (p. 125).

It is Mrs Hayward, and they follow her. The Lanes are described: 'All summer afternoons in the Lanes seem to labour under a kind of hot dullness and heaviness' (pp. 125–26); 'choking green torpor' (p. 126); 'another, more ancient and frightening land' (p. 126). They pass the Cottages. Note the description of the children on pp. 126–27; the working-class inhabitants of the Cottages are completely beyond their comprehension. They can deal with German spies, but not the underclass.

They arrive at 'the Barns', the desolate area marked out for development but abandoned on the outbreak of war — including collapsed farm buildings. A staircase leads down under a sheet of corrugated iron. 'We've come on a journey from the highest to the lowest — from the silver-framed heroes on the altars in the Haywards' house…to an old derelict taking refuge under a sheet of corrugated iron in a stinking elder bush, without even a dog to speak up for him' (p. 130). (Note the unsubtle **irony**, as it is the same person being referred to.) They hear the 'tramp' coughing down below the corrugated iron sheets, and they beat on it with sticks. (Why? It is Stephen who starts it, but no explanation is given; this is bullying, but they do not recognise it as such.) Then they stop laughing (they remember a similar incident, the bullying of Eddie Stott) and run away. They dare not go down to investigate. They leave 'that skulking, ancient land beyond the tunnel' (p. 132). They return and find Keith's father waiting for Keith's mother — and they both realise that she must have been down there with the tramp. Nothing is said until Stephen leaves, and Mrs Hayward says, in despair, 'Was it you two?…Oh, Stephen' (p. 133).

Chapter 7 (pp. 137–48) — viewpoint: present day initially, then past

Clearly, at this point Mrs Hayward assumes that the boys, as a result of following her (and despite her request to Stephen that they should not), now understand who it is that she is visiting. Old Stephen reasonably asks: 'So how much did Stephen understand at this point about what was going on?' (p. 137) — a device to re-distance the reader from the wartime narrative. And he begins to unravel the confusion of Stephen's thoughts at the time: 'the clean simplicity of espionage, that had promised so well, had turned into such a sticky mess' (p. 141).

On p. 142 the narrative reverts to the past. Keith does not come out to play for some days. Finally Stephen summons courage to go over there again. Mrs Hayward is her old self again. Stephen goes up to Keith's room: 'He's telling me the game's over [note the irony]. The question of his mother's espionage, which once seemed so urgent, has turned out to be too difficult to resolve' (p. 142).

But Keith is busy about his chores; they do not talk of the great project which has been abandoned, nor of any other: 'It's not just the one game that's over; all our games are over' (p. 144).

Then Keith's father accuses him of having taken the thermos flask from the picnic basket. Keith is taken into the house and his hands are beaten. When they emerge, his father says 'And your mother's at Auntie Dee's again?' — as if he is uneasy about it now (p. 146).

Stephen resolves to put matters right, somehow, and runs through the tunnel — colliding with Mrs Hayward, who is initially angry until he is able to say 'The thermos flask!' (p. 148). She realises, reconstructs what will have happened, and is humbled. She sets out back to the Barns — and thanks Stephen.

References and allusions

p. 145, thermos flask. An insulated flask used to keep drinks hot, an essential part of a picnic kit of the period.

p. 147, chassé. A formal step in a dance.

Chapter 8 (pp. 151–71) — viewpoint: entirely in the past

'What's going to happen now?' asks the framework narrator (p. 151). Note that midsummer is approaching (p. 151). Keith's house is now closed to Stephen. He does not know what to do. He wants to tell a grown-up, but his schoolboy code prevents him: 'It's telling tales, there's no getting away from it' (p. 153). Sitting disconsolately in the look-out, Stephen is joined by Barbara Berrill — who once again knows more than Stephen does. This time, it is that Mrs Hayward no longer goes to Auntie Dee's, but that Keith does the shopping instead — as they observe together. Barbara gives a running commentary, having effortlessly taken over the role of leader given up by Keith. They see Mrs Hayward emerge with letters, Mr Hayward stop her, and then accompany her to the post. But something is wrong with Mrs Hayward's sandal, and she returns to the house, leaving Mr Hayward to post the letters — all but the one she has kept. She comes over to ask Stephen to take it — but sees that Barbara is there, and dare not. But Barbara knows anyway: 'She wanted you to take him that letter, didn't she?' (p. 157) — whoever Barbara thinks 'him' might be.

The next day a policeman visits Auntie Dee, and then Mrs Hayward. The younger children of the street function as a kind of chorus, commenting on the action. Stephen is with them, as is Barbara Berrill, but they both say nothing. Various rumours fly, principally that the 'peeping Tom' was seen again the previous night. Afterwards, Barbara confides to Stephen what Deirdre and Geoffrey were up to last night: '"They kiss each other," she whispers. "Deirdre told me. They smoke cigarettes and then they kiss each other"' (p. 163). Then, lying across his lap, she insists on opening the trunk. Stephen gives her the key; she tries to smoke a cigarette butt. Stephen tries: 'It tastes of importance and of being grown up' (p. 166). Then, a key paragraph, beginning 'as if I'm no longer bound by the rules and restrictions of childhood' (pp. 166–67) shows that he is beginning to grow out of Keith and his childish games. It then occurs to Stephen that the butt they've been smoking may have been left by *him* (a packet of tipped 'Craven A' cigarettes was in the croquet box). 'And now everything has changed once again' (p. 168). The first mention is made of 'Lamorna' (the name of Barbara Berrill's house, but with much wider associations; see 'Images, symbols and motifs' on p. 64 of this guide). 'I see all kinds of things I never saw before' (p. 169). He also, at last, refers to Battle of Britain vapour trails ('an earlier summer sky', p. 169) and sirens and searchlights. He thinks he has finally worked out what has happened: it is a parachuted German airman on whom Mrs Hayward has taken pity.

References and allusions

p. 168, Lamorna. A cove in Cornwall, and also a folk-song set there; the name of Barbara Berrill's house. It summons up a **lyrical** sound of mourning and nostalgia.

Chapter 9 (pp. 175–96) — viewpoint: present day initially, then past

The chapter begins in the present day again, looking back, reconstructing. The narrator recalls that the situation had changed, and so had Mrs Hayward: 'I think she seemed somehow even more perfect than before…an air of regal haughtiness' (p. 175). 'Only now do I realise' he says, a key theme of the book (p. 175). He attempts to reconstruct how Mrs Hayward asked young Stephen to take the basket to the Barns. (Note that Frayn chooses not to relive this key scene, instead summarising it from the present; why? And why can Stephen be asked to do this, whereas Keith cannot? The question is not addressed, but the reason must be that she does not feel she can trust Keith. This may hint at a deeper difficulty in their relationship, which is never discussed.)

Finally, he reverts to the narrative. Mrs Hayward explains that 'he' was ill, and had no ration book and so needed the things in the basket. She calls Stephen 'darling' as she says 'I can't explain' (p. 177). She assumes that he knows who it is: 'Anyway, I think you *do* understand' (p. 177). She persuasively explains about boys being bullied at school, obviously referring to him, and he knows it's about him and his ears (p. 177). She nearly breaks down: 'I feel so…So ashamed' (p. 178). He feebly suggests Auntie Dee, but then realises that it must have been she who first found the 'German' (hence all the rumours of her having a boyfriend). And Stephen begins to

realise that he has some responsibility in all this: 'I realise that the very things that seemed so simple and straightforward then are not so simple and straightforward at all, but infinitely complex and painful' (p. 179). And he begins to appreciate that his childish intervention has had consequences. He says, 'Just by looking at things I shouldn't have looked at, I've changed them' (p. 179), because, by finding the croquet box, he has forced Mrs Hayward to go all the way to the Barns to take things. But then Mrs Hayward starts to say more: 'Yes, that's what we used to do…I used to look after Milly while Dee went' (p. 180); 'Life can be so cruel sometimes. It all seems so easy for a start. And then…' (p. 180). She then makes the key statement:

> When you and Keith started your little game of detectives…when you began looking in my things and following me around, I don't suppose it ever occurred to you that it would all end up like this, with me crying on your shoulder. Poor Stephen! It was a naughty thing to do, you know, spying on people.

Stephen has failed to respond throughout all this, and she assumes he is refusing. But she now thinks Stephen understands: 'now you know who it is' (p. 181). But he still does not. He does, however, agree to take the basket. The privet is now blossoming white, with its distinctive (and unpleasant) smell. And for Stephen, sitting in the middle of it, it is bound up with so many new sensations — and Lamorna.

Before he can take the basket, Barbara has materialised, having seen everything. Stephen is confused, and Barbara is hostile, but finally she produces a cigarette and they smoke it together. 'Our quarrel has apparently ended in perfect agreement' (p. 85). They had argued over whether to look in the basket, but in the end Stephen does not stop her. The basket mostly contains food, plus some medicine left over from a recent illness of Keith's. There is also a sealed envelope, which they do not open. Then Barbara kisses him. He is surprised: it is a sign of his upbringing that his reaction is 'I hadn't really got round to thinking about whether it was nice or not. I was too busy thinking about the germs' (p. 186). Barbara then lies on him — to take the bayonet and slit the letter open. At that moment Mr Hayward appears, calls Stephen 'old chap' and demands the basket. They both go back to the Haywards' garage. Mr Hayward tersely says: 'Word of advice, old fellow…Silly games. Don't play them' (p. 187). He orders Stephen to hand the basket over — but he refuses until Mr Hayward says please. At that moment, Mrs Hayward arrives; there is a moment of extreme tension, highlighting the brittle and unnatural relationship of the two Haywards. Mrs Hayward covers; Stephen runs off home: 'I'm running home to Mummy. My life's over' (p. 190).

Unable to sleep, he notes that it is the last day of the moon's cycle. He thinks of the 'German' airman: 'All around him, mocking his loneliness, is the sweet reek of some intangible happiness, and the faint, melancholy notes of an old sad song called "Lamorna"' (p. 192).

The next morning he resolves that 'I have to make one more attempt to redeem all my failures — and this time I have to succeed' (p. 193). He fills his satchel with spare food (from the cupboard under the stairs where they slept 'during the worst of the raids', p. 193) and sets out 'on that horrible journey' (p. 194). He passes the 'disheartening landmarks' (p. 194) which make it seem like a journey into the underworld — a metaphor Frayn then uses on p. 196:

> I think of Keith's mother, coming out of the world of silver ornaments and silver chimes and descending the great ladder of the world, rung by rung, until she finds herself where I'm standing, in the smell of the elders and the excrement — and then going on, further down, into the underworld.

He empties his satchel, and is about to leave when the voice from the darkness says 'Stephen?' (p. 196).

References and allusions

p. 185, M & B tablets. New sulphonamide drugs, named after the makers, May and Baker.

p. 192, 'Lamorna'. The words are:

> Soa now I'll sing to ee,
> Tes abowt a maiden fair
> I met tha oather aevenen
> en tha corner of tha square.
> She ad a dark an roven eye,
> she waz a charmen roaver,
> An we road oll night
> En tha pale moonlight
> Awae down t' Lamorna.
>
> Twas down en Albert Square
> I neer er shall forgit,
> er eyes they shoan like dymons
> an tha eavenen et was wit, wit, wit.
> Er air ung down en curls,
> she was a charmen roaver,
> An we road oll night
> En tha pale moonlight
> Awae down t' Lamorna
>
> Az we got en tha cab
> I axed er fer er naem,
> An wen she givd et me,
> Well mine et woz tha saem.
> Soa I lefted up er veil,
> Fer er faes woz coavered oaver;
> T'my surprise
> It woz me wife
> I'd road down t' Lamorna.

She said, I knawed ee well,
I nawd ee all tha while,
I nawd you en tha dark
An I did un fer a lark,
An fer that lark you'll pay
Fer that roven of yer donor.
You'll pay tha fare,
I do declare,
Awae down t' Lamorna.

Chapter 10 (pp. 199–222) — viewpoint: present day initially, then past

The chapter starts, yet again, in the present with a rhetorical question: 'Did Stephen understand at last who it was down there…?' (p. 199). And the narrator does not know the answer, because Stephen 'might both know and yet not know' (p. 199) as the 'tramp' questions him: 'Was it Bobs who sent you?' (p. 200).

An unreal conversation ensues, in which the 'tramp' assumes that Stephen knows who he is, and Stephen clings with increasing implausibility to his belief that the 'tramp' is a parachuted German — even though he speaks perfect English and knows them all by name. Finally, he reveals what happened — the breakdown on a mission (p. 203). Still Stephen claims not to understand.

Note the repeated references to the power of duty instilled in a middle-class boy of the period: 'still helplessly obedient to adult authority' (p. 201), 'There's nothing for it but to obey' (p. 204).

Then comes the real revelation: 'It was always her, you know…From the very beginning. Always her' (p. 205; but Stephen does not understand, although the audience does). Following this, and his failure to write her a note, he hands over his scarf, saying 'And tell her…tell her…' (a direct echo of *The Go-Between*) — 'Tell her "for ever"' (p. 205).

Stephen becomes sentimental: 'Lamorna sounded like waves lapping softly on the shore; "for ever" sounds like a key turning softly through the wards of a well-oiled lock' (p. 205).

The scarf is a silk escape map (although Stephen does not realise this), and he reads 'Chemnitz…Leipzig…Zwickau' (p. 206), which, ironically, confirms for Stephen that the 'tramp' is a German, despite all the other evidence which he is ignoring. He returns to the lookout — and finds that Barbara has tidied it; his feelings are mixed (p. 206). He sees that Auntie Dee is visiting Mrs Hayward, and watches them talk before Dee leaves. Then, against his expectations, for the first time for 'at least two weeks', there is Keith in the lookout (p. 208). He has found that Barbara has been in the trunk — and puts the bayonet to Stephen's throat, and quietly cuts it. But Stephen does not give him the map. Keith dismissively says 'Do what you like, then, old bean…Play houses with your girlfriend if you want to. I don't care' (p.212).

Stephen goes home, and his injured neck is seen. He will not tell his parents who it was, but they guess; Geoff finds the rations gone.

That night, he goes out to hide the scarf beside the embankment, where the croquet box used to be. But two men arrive in a truck and climb past him onto the track; they collect something (a body) as other men approach from the Lanes. They take it away. Stephen assumes it is the 'tramp', killed on the rails (by the third-rail electric current). He briefly saw parts of damaged aircraft on the stationary train above. 'The game's finally over', he claims (p. 222) — but how often has he ended a chapter on such a note?

References and allusions

p. 203, a dicky engine. Not functioning properly.

p. 205, the wards of a well-oiled lock. 'Wards' are the moving parts of a lock mechanism.

p. 206, Chemnitz…Leipzig…Zwickau. Uncle Peter has given Stephen his silk escape map, issued to all bomber crews operating over Germany. They were printed by Waddingtons (the game manufacturer) and could be concealed in the lining of a flying jacket. Chemnitz, Leipzig and Zwickau were all major cities in the east of Germany, and regular raids on these cities began only late on in the war.

p. 208, your Ena Harkness. A classic rose (with a brilliant red double blossom) (note the frequent references to 'the standard roses', also on p. 208).

p. 221, the clanking of tightened couplings. Couplings link together the wagons of a goods train. When a train starts, the couplings extend to their maximum with a metallic clanking sound.

Chapter 11 (pp. 225–34) — viewpoint: present day

This final chapter is told entirely from the present day; the omniscient narrator is immersed in nostalgia for the past; not quite self-pity, but close. Everything is finally revealed. He never went back to Keith's house; he never, surprisingly, went to the hideout again; but Barbara Berrill had moved on to another boy in the street. Uncle Peter was posted missing, and Auntie Dee moved away. Keith went off to boarding school (but would have returned every holiday).

More revealingly, it turns out that he is actually Stefan Weitzler, Jewish-German refugee, and that he returned to Germany (probably Berlin) in the 1960s following the deaths of his parents. He suffered from 'a great restlessness' (p. 229) and found a 'home' very like the 'home' he had in the Close.

And finally, he says 'Did I really not know at the time that the broken man in the Barns was Uncle Peter? Of course I knew. I knew as soon as he called me by name ' (p. 233) — or even earlier. He is able to reveal no more at all about what

actually happened in Chapter 10; we presume that Uncle Peter had run away, onto the tracks, and had been killed by a train. Did he kill himself? Or was he running away? Where?

References and allusions

p. 227, too weeny, too weedy, and too Wheatley. An echo of the Latin phrase that all prep school boys were required to learn ('Veni, vidi, vici', pronounced 'weni, widi, wiki', words attributed to Julius Caesar when he landed in Britain in 54 BC, meaning 'I came, I saw, I conquered.'

Characters

Stephen and Keith

The relationship between Stephen and Keith lies at the heart of the novel. We are never explicitly told their age, and the reader must form a judgement; they are clearly at that awkward stage where they are still children, content to play children's make-believe games, but are beginning to glimpse and struggle towards a more adolescent viewpoint. Stephen's elder brother Geoff stands for the stage they will no doubt arrive at soon enough; he has put aside boyish games in favour of smoking and girlfriends. During this summer of transformation, Stephen takes his first faltering steps towards both of these things, although for Keith they remain unimaginably alien, perhaps because he is an only child (p. 17: 'no stupid brothers or sisters').

The boys are first presented to the reader in Chapter 2, and the contrast in the initial images sets up the unequal relationship between them. Stephen is presented in a strange and unsettling way, which prepares the reader for the curious relationship between the narrator and young Stephen throughout the book. He is viewed from the outside, as if there were no connection between the narrator and his younger self — an artificial distancing mechanism:

> But is that the way that he sees it at his age? I mean the awkward boy who lives
> in that unkempt house between the Hardiments and the Pinchers — Stephen
> Wheatley, the one with the stick-out ears and the too-short grey flannel school
> shirt hanging out of the too-long grey flannel school shorts. (p. 12)

The narrator claims to 'watch him emerge', as if the boy is so completely separate from him that he can actually observe him. It is a strange fiction and colours our view of the boy: the narrator is consistently self-deprecating — or rather, Stephen-deprecating; but is it just a device? We are not given a physical description, except for the ears; only the clothes, the external details, are reported, i.e. the features that the bullies see.

Keith, as seen by the impressionable and inferior Stephen (then and/or now?), is clean, smart, superior: the ideal middle-class prep-school boy. We first see him on pp. 14–15, as though we were standing beside the older Stephen at the side of the younger Stephen, waiting at the door of 'Chollerton', the pretentiously named house in which Keith lives: 'a boy of Stephen's age…His shirt, though, is not too short, his shorts are not too long. His grey socks are neatly pulled up to half an inch below his knees, and his brown leather sandals are neatly buckled' (pp. 14–15). Note that this is a description of clothing again, rather than of the boy. A description of the house follows. When the narrator returns to Keith, it is to more detail of his clothing — 'We're socially colour-coded for ease of reference' (p. 15). Note that conformity of clothing was of great importance to children, then as now; the difference is humiliating for Stephen. He summarises: 'The Haywards were impeccable' (p. 23).

Note the impression made by the boys' surnames: both reflect traditional countryside occupations (to stress the recency of the move to the town?), but whereas 'Hayward' may echo the responsible idea of 'warding' (guarding) the hay, 'Wheatley' (wheat) is similar to 'weak', as the bullies immediately pick up.

The inequality of the relationship is immediately established by the self-mocking 'He was the officer corps in our two-man army. I was the Other Ranks — and grateful to be so' (p. 16). In Britain at that time, there was an unbridgeable social gulf between officers and other ranks. He continues:

> We had a great many enterprises and projects in hand, and in all of them he was the leader and I was the led. I see now that he was only the first in a whole series of dominant figures in my life whose disciple I became.

Note the implication of the word 'disciple' — that Keith was not merely a leader, but messiah-like. 'His authority was entirely warranted by his intellectual and imaginative superiority' (p. 16).

As the novel progresses, so the relationship between Stephen and Keith emerges more clearly. It remains a question whether it actually develops, or remains fundamentally the same throughout. It can be argued that it changes very little. When Keith cuts Stephen off later in the novel, Stephen does not question the nature of the relationship, but merely mourns Keith's absence. The reader, of course, notices that Stephen becomes more independent with Keith out of the way, daring to chat to Barbara Berrill, breaking Keith's authoritarian rules (in the mould of Keith's father) and even doing a deal with Mrs Hayward. When Keith reappears, however, Stephen immediately and without question reverts to subservience and the relationship resumes as if nothing had happened. Note that during the interlude of Keith's absence, Barbara Berrill effortlessly takes over the role of all-knowing leader; it is as if Stephen is grateful to be led (Chapter 8).

Keith reappears on p. 208. It has been more than two weeks — an unimaginable length of time for them to be apart — but although things may look the same, they have changed. Stephen decides not to show him the scarf; and Keith is angry that Stephen has broken his oath by showing things to Barbara. He ends up cutting

Stephen's throat — and Stephen can see that he has changed: 'They're the eyes of a stranger' (p. 210). But Stephen accepts Keith's right to hurt him, without serious protest. Tellingly, Keith dismisses the change in Stephen: 'Play houses with your girlfriend if you want to' (p. 212). Keith, it seems, has no intention of growing up in the way that Stephen has begun to — perhaps because many of his values, assimilated from his father, are already middle-aged. Keith seems to be mutating into his father in this final, estranged section. 'He smiles his father's thin smile' and he uses the words 'old bean' (p. 209).

Young Stephen

Young Stephen is a nervous and diffident child. He prefers to follow rather than to lead, and is prepared to be led anywhere — as long as it does not conflict with the values that have been inculcated in him by his middle-class parents. He is fearful and is used to being bullied. Nevertheless, he shows some independence as the events develop, although it could be argued that he is simply following the orders of a new leader (Barbara) over those of an earlier one (Keith). He is fundamentally decent and is quite sensitive; he empathises with the plight of several other characters at times, especially Mrs Hayward, whom he is forced to see in a new light after she has thrown herself upon Stephen's mercy. He can be quite determined, when he has made up his mind, and quite brave — he goes to the Barns alone, for example. But fear and the desire to impress others are often the deciding emotions. Although he is dismissive of his parents, he knows that they care about him and are unlikely to beat him in the way that Keith's father is prepared to beat Keith.

Stephen's reactions when embarrassed, caught out or put under pressure are revealing indicators of his character. He is a truthful, well brought-up middle-class boy who has internalised the 'code of honour' that lying is unacceptable. Because he allows himself to be led by Keith into situations that are not of his choosing, however, he frequently finds that he cannot or dare not tell the truth. (The elder Stephen seems to be suggesting that if only he could have been more assertive, he might have been able to avoid these situations.) Stephen's most characteristic reaction in such cases is to remain silent, as if struck dumb. This is his preferred method for avoiding incriminating or explaining himself. It is exploited by Keith, who makes him swear never to divulge what they are doing. Stephen returns wet from the Lanes, for example, and is questioned by his family: 'I say nothing' (p. 119). Then: 'But here I revert to total uncommunicativeness. Am I deliberately refusing to speak about things that I know must never be revealed to outsiders? Or am I simply too shocked to open my mouth?' (p. 119). When Mrs Hayward asked him to take the basket, 'Stephen kept his eyes on the ground and said nothing' (p. 177). When Mr Hayward has summoned him to the garage to hand over the basket, Stephen refuses to speak to him: 'Silence' (p. 187). After Keith has cut his throat with the knife, Stephen is again interrogated by his concerned family; over and over, 'I say nothing', 'Silence', etc (p. 213–14).

Keith

Keith is a very repressed boy. As an only child, he is unable to resist the authoritarian, disciplined climate established by his repressed and repressive father, although he is spoiled by his mother. He takes it out on Stephen — but in a similar, highly repressed way. Although immature in some ways (e.g. his complete indifference to girls, his determination to play childish make-believe games, which exasperate his mother), he also behaves like a middle-aged man. His room is always tidy, he imposes rigid rules on those about him, and he displays no spontaneity at all. He lives in fear of his father, knowing that the threats to cane him, so casually made, will be carried out if he fails in any way to comply with the rigid rules imposed upon him. When, in Chapter 7, Keith is suspected of having taken the thermos flask, his father displays almost no emotion in telling him to go inside and prepare his hands for a beating. Afterwards he simply says 'If it's not back by then you'll get the same again. And then again tomorrow. And so on every day until it's back' (p. 146). Nor, in his turn, does Keith display any emotion, merely parroting his father's idiom when he says to Stephen 'I told you to go, old bean.' It is possible that the shame of having Stephen witness his humiliation in this way contributes to the cold, unemotional way in which he, in his turn, inflicts pain on Stephen by cutting his throat in Chapter 10.

Other characters

Old Stephen (the narrator)

Old Stephen initially defines himself in terms of 'restlessness' and 'homesickness' for the home of his childhood (p. 3). His remote attitude to young Stephen is a deliberate distancing device, and serves to conceal the character of old Stephen. He initially seems rather mild and timid, as he tentatively remakes his acquaintance with the places of his childhood. His teasing of the reader immediately gives the impression that he likes power, however, and possibly enjoys manipulation. He is self-deprecating almost immediately: 'I see now that he was only the first in a whole series of dominant figures in my life whose disciple I became' (p. 16). Old Stephen continues to tease us throughout the novel, and by the end the reader may be quite annoyed by the way in which he has withheld information.

Beyond that, he emerges as a rather gentle, unpretentious, sentimental man. A follower rather than a leader, he has probably always been timid; it is instructive that when he saw the name 'K. R. G. Hayward' he was held back by 'some last residual fear' (p. 232) from confronting him. He is a curious mixture of manipulator and victim. He expresses 'Gratitude…to all the others…whose adjutant and audience I was' (p. 29).

Old Stephen implies that the experiences described in the novel had a lasting (and, by implication, damaging) effect upon Stephen's ability to become an independent and confident adult.

He also suggests that this was not really Keith's fault, but rather that the fault lay in young Stephen. He often states that it was in young Stephen's personality to be led; he was happy to be Keith's follower. He also immediately accepts the dominant role played by Barbara, and he unquestioningly accepts the authority of all adults (although he often avoids answering their questions). As the novel progresses, Stephen becomes increasingly able to defy Keith and his wishes — with Barbara, in agreeing to Mrs Hayward's demands, giving in to Mr Hayward, and, most surprising and significant, not showing the scarf to Keith, even though this might have won back Keith's favour and avoided the throat-cutting. But Stephen has moved on from his days of utter dependence in this summer of transition, partly thanks to Barbara. In the end, it is Keith who is shown to be the inadequate one, locked into childish games, repressed by his father, and capable of violence. Stephen has, to a limited extent, adapted and grown up.

It is therefore an interesting question why old Stephen thinks that the events of this early summer have exercised such a hold upon him that he has to return to the site and, as it were, exorcise its ghosts. Unlike Leo in *The Go-Between*, who is so traumatised that he cannot form a relationship thereafter, Stephen seems merely to have lost a friend and moved on. He has managed to marry, to find a moderately satisfying job (eventually), and to take the decision to return to Germany. Perhaps the summer marked the high point of his life, in that he was at the heart of events, appealed to by so many adults, playing an important role in serious matters — and the remainder of his humdrum life was an anti-climax afterwards.

Mrs Hayward

We first see Mrs Hayward as an exalted being into whose presence Stephen is shown to take his leave at the end of a visit (pp. 28–29); she is alone, surrounded by evidence of her status ('a silver teapot, a silver milk jug, and a little silver box containing tiny pills of saccharine', p. 29), and unapproachable. By the end of the same chapter, however, Keith has announced 'My mother…is a German spy' (p. 33), clouding the image considerably.

During the course of the novel our view of Mrs Hayward develops a great deal. Although she plays the socially superior wife quite skilfully, she is obviously lonely, enjoys the company of her sister, and hides complex emotions behind her rather rigid middle-class mask. She is shown to be compassionate over Uncle Peter's fate (we never know whether she knew, consciously or otherwise, his true feelings for her, revealed on p. 205); and although aloof, she shows a human side on several occasions, principally when Stephen encounters her and mentions the thermos flask, as she realises what must have happened to Keith. She is actually quite soft towards Stephen (unlike her husband, who refuses to acknowledge him at all). On pp. 179–81 we see her at her most vulnerable when asking Stephen for a favour.

She is actually called 'Bobs', but we do not learn this until Uncle Peter refers to her by this name on p. 200; to Stephen she is always 'Mrs Hayward' or 'Keith's mother', as befits an adult. We are not told what 'Bobs' is an abbreviation for (she was 'R. J. Whitman' before marriage, p. 28), and her husband is never heard to call her by name.

One unresolved question concerns what actually happened with Peter when she went to visit him in the Barns. Several commentators refer to her 'adultery', but there is no evidence in the novel that anything of the sort happened; indeed, Peter's final message to her strongly suggests that he believes she still does not realise the intensity of his feelings for her. It is possible that Mr Hayward believes that adulterous behaviour took place, however, if it led him to cut her throat.

Mr Hayward

Mr Hayward is introduced in Chapter 2 as a kind of paragon in young Stephen's eyes, but a very inhuman one in the reader's. He does not work (although this is not explained), but is clearly obsessive about routine and cleanliness: 'for ever making perfection yet more perfect' (p. 20). His clipped utterances are formal to the point of being comic, e.g. 'Door — paint — wet' (p. 22) or 'Bike away in the shed, old boy' (p. 22). Stephen holds him in awe, both as a war hero (an officer, he killed five Germans with his legendary bayonet during the Great War) and as a terrifying authority figure. He refuses to acknowledge Stephen's existence, and his relationship with Keith is very formal: 'he had to go and ask his father for permission to walk on the lawn' (p. 21); 'if that toy aeroplane of yours touches the greenhouse, old bean…I'll cane you' (p. 22).

Mr Hayward's reserve and distance are put under pressure by the events that follow. When he is forced eventually to speak to Stephen (in Chapter 9), he attempts to bully him; his threats are shown to be empty, however, when his bluff is called. He becomes seriously concerned about his wife (genuine, or only because of how it might look to others?) and begins to issue orders to her as well.

We are told that he was an 'unsociable, middle-aged husband' (p. 233) when Peter dated Dee back in 1929 (p. 28), so it is possible that now, 15 years later, he has retired; this would explain why he does nothing but potter around in the garden, and also his distant and formal relationship with his son. He was old enough to fight in the Great War. He is a bit of a **stereotype**, in his clipped utterances: 'Word of advice, old fellow…Silly games. Don't play them' (p. 187). It should be noted, though, that it was not uncommon at the time for middle-class fathers to display signs of emotional and linguistic atrophy, having been encouraged by the values of the period to conceal their emotions at all times and keep a 'stiff upper lip.'

Mr and Mrs Hayward as a couple

Although they are presented as a perfect middle-class couple, the reality is that the Haywards seem to lead entirely separate lives. Mrs Hayward has a life with her sister (and, occasionally, Uncle Peter); the rest of the time she is in the house, reading, writing or sleeping. Mr Hayward is invariably in the garden or garage. He may in fact (although young Stephen does not seem to notice this) be significantly older than her. Why do they have only one child? This is never referred to, but the infrequency of the exclamation marks in Mrs Hayward's diary suggest that their conjugal moments are rare. He obviously has an obsessive, controlling personality; it seems that Mrs Hayward has carved out her area of independent action, but when things go wrong he tightens his control over her.

Equally, the fact that she feels unable to confide in him about what has happened with Uncle Peter suggests a fundamental weakness in their relationship. Does she not trust his possibly extreme reaction? As an acknowledged 'hero', might he denounce Peter as a weakling and failure, or even a traitor? Does she fear his temper, or the risk that he will suspect/realise her feelings for Peter?

He shows, at the crisis, that he in turn does not trust his wife (arguably with good reason, as she has been engaging in an elaborate and extended deception to conceal what she has really been doing); and surely his obsession with cleanliness, and with routine, conceals frustration (this is a literary and psychoanalytical stereotype). Does he suspect that Mrs Hayward really cares more about Peter and would rather have married him?

If, as is implied, he inflicted physical harm on her at the crisis (see p. 211), that is evidence of his potential for violence.

Barbara Berrill

Barbara is introduced by Stephen thus: 'as sly and treacherous as most girls are' (p. 13) — both a dismissal and a **stereotype** revealing his immaturity. When Barbara first intrudes on Stephen on p. 96, she is presented in a way that emphasises his feeling that girls are alien: 'there's something girlishly self-satisfied about the bobbliness of the leather and the shininess of the popper'. Although she annoys him, it is clear that she has a level of understanding that surpasses his, and his attempts to hide his ignorance merely show him up further. She is seen with the dismissive eyes of a boy who has not yet entered adolescence. We are given no indication of whether she is, or Stephen thinks her to be, attractive; as with virtually all the characters in the book, the only description is of her clothes.

As Barbara makes a determined effort to break down Stephen's hostility, he finds himself, despite his own wishes, being drawn to her. She acts as a catalyst, helping him to place his relationship with Keith in perspective, and offering a glimpse of a more adult world that awaits him just as soon as he can break out of childhood. She seizes the initiative and forces Stephen to move faster than he wishes to, although he does not regret it. He acknowledges that she is simply replacing Keith as a leader whom he follows. However, her motives must be questioned; she seems to enjoy showing off her (invariably superior) knowledge of what is going on in the street, and the fact is that she loses interest in Stephen as soon as the Uncle Peter episode is concluded. Although (perhaps because?) he subsequently takes the initiative and tries to see her, she has already moved on: 'I called at Lamorna several times, but Barbara could never come out to play' (p. 228). The suspicion must be that her real interest was in penetrating the boys' hideout, breaking up their blood-friendship and getting access to the locked trunk, which she had no doubt found on one of her snooping expeditions. Stephen shows no sign, however, of feeling put out by her double dealing.

Uncle Peter

Uncle Peter is introduced in hagiographical terms, i.e. as though he were a saint: 'the glory of Uncle Peter' (p. 25). He is an archetypal RAF war hero, characterised by phrases such as 'his cheerful bravery' and 'his careless disregard for danger' (p. 25). As he is absent, there is no possibility of a corrective.

Peter Tracey (as he is never called) is the linch-pin of the plot, but he is virtually never seen and when he is he is not identified. This makes him an elusive figure, but nevertheless it is clear that he subverts the stereotype of a hero. His nerve has broken, and he is found skulking in an underground shelter. He has returned to be near his wife, and is suffering from a breakdown in his health to match his nervous breakdown. We never really understand what happened to him, and crucially we do not understand why he leaves the bunker at the end of the novel to be killed on the railway tracks. He is evidently a complex and tortured personality, admitting at the last (in the surreal conversation with Stephen when the latter pretends not to know who he really is) 'It was always her, you know…From the very beginning. Always her' (p. 205) — meaning Mrs Hayward, not Auntie Dee. The wild way in which he begs Stephen to 'Tell her "for ever"' (p. 205) gives an indication of his final state of mind, and suggests that he had concluded that the only way out was for him to kill himself. We never learn whether this is true.

Mr Wheatley (Stephen's father)

'The presence of Stephen's father was scarcely noticeable' (p. 26); 'He often seemed like some mild-natured furry animal' (p. 26). He is gentle and sympathetic when Stephen is bullied at school, but is not really a presence in the novel: 'Once he'd been away on some business trip in the North for a whole year, and no one had ever talked about it or even noticed particularly' (p. 26). At the end, of course, we discover a very different story; as a Jewish refugee from Nazi Germany, he knew well enough about persecution, and the work he was engaged in was far less dull than Stephen imagined.

Mrs Wheatley (Stephen's mother)

'There's something so hopelessly ordinary about her that it's difficult to take account of her existence' (p. 42). It is confirmed at the end of the novel that she was genuinely

English (p. 228), making it easier for her husband, Herr Weitzler, to move to Britain. She is gentle and concerned about Stephen.

Geoff Wheatley

Geoff is also a cipher, an archetypal elder brother with whom Stephen seems to have very little to do, even though he shares a room with him. His introduction as Stephen's 'insufferable elder brother' (p. 13) clearly sets the tone, although in reality he does not appear to treat Stephen particularly badly.

Auntie Dee

Auntie Dee ought to be an interesting and complex character, given the ambiguous role she plays in the novel. At what point, for example, does she become aware that her husband is really in love with her elder sister? It is implied that, at an early stage of his exile in the Barns, she used to meet Peter under the bridge ('Mrs Tracey's boyfriend', Barbara calls him on p. 101), but later she seems to have been content for her sister to conduct all communication with him. Why? And what did she imagine they did there? How did she feel about the whole business? All this is not revealed, although we are told that she moved out of the district shortly after Peter's death — presumably thereby severing links with her sister.

She is introduced in Chapter 2 as 'yet another amazing ornament of the Hayward family' (p. 23), in Stephen's view, although she is of course nothing to do with the Hayward family (she must have been born a Whitman, and became Mrs Tracey). She has a young daughter, Milly, who perhaps prevents her from playing a more active role in the events. Dee is rarely seen directly in the novel, and when she is, it is her smile that makes the greatest impression on Stephen: 'No one could smile like that and have any secrets from the world' (p. 103). This comment, of course, reinforces the naivety of Stephen's observations.

Children, adults and coming of age

The relationships between children and adults form an important aspect of the novel. The adults act in the real world, whereas the children mimic adult actions in their childish fantasy world. Because they do not fully understand the significance of adult actions and interactions, their interference runs the risk of having unforeseen and potentially damaging consequences. Arguably, it is finding out the adult results of his childish games that enables Stephen to begin the journey to adulthood.

The ages of Stephen and Keith are not given at any point in the novel. We do, however, know that they are still at prep school and have not yet taken Common

Entrance, the exam for entry to senior school, typically taken at 13. They have not arrived at an age where they are interested in girls and smoking, although Stephen is aware of them (through his brother Geoff; Keith, with no brother, is less advanced). They might therefore be 12 or 13, especially as we are told that Keith goes off to his new school in the September following the events of the novel. They are still happy to play children's games, although perhaps with an element of self-consciousness and incongruity.

The attitude of the adults to the two boys differs significantly. Stephen's parents are sympathetic to him. They know he is bullied and wish to support him. They are not judgemental, and do not try to make him grow up prematurely. When he returns injured, they are angry and compassionate and immediately suspect Keith (p. 213). Stephen's mother is happy for him to live in the world of his childish games but underestimates how he is beginning to grow up. The true status of his parents as refugees from persecution, revealed only in the final chapter, may help to explain this attitude.

The attitude of Keith's parents is quite different. His father is distant, and mostly speaks to Keith to give an order or to remind him of a prohibition. Keith does not dare question these rules, because he knows the likely consequences. When, through no fault of his, the thermos flask goes missing, his father beats him without the slightest sign of emotion. It is clear from Keith's lack of reaction that this has happened many times before. His mother, by contrast, generally indulges Keith; she does not need to make rules, because she knows her husband will do that. However, it is interesting that she opts to trust Stephen rather than Keith at the crisis; perhaps she suspects that Keith's fear of his father makes him an unreliable accomplice.

Keith never goes to Stephen's house. The behaviour of Keith's parents towards Stephen is odd, in that they refuse to speak to him, instead using Keith as a channel. Keith knows that punishment will ensue if there is any deviation from the rules. However, the events of the summer require both of the Haywards to speak to Stephen directly, Mrs Hayward in Chapter 5 for the first time, and, even more shockingly, Mr Hayward when he confronts Stephen over the basket in Chapter 9.

It is noteworthy that both of Keith's parents are exasperated by the make-believe games he plays. 'Even the best of games can sometimes get a bit out of hand' (p. 107), Mrs Hayward says, and Mr Hayward dismisses them as 'silly games of let's-pretend' (p. 187). It is also interesting that Keith's mother, to Stephen's incredulity, believes that 'Keith's easily led' (p. 108). Mrs Hayward's decision to trust Stephen and confide in him gives evidence that, although she seemed barely aware of him earlier, she has in fact been watching and judging him.

The novel is set in the summer in which Stephen begins the transition from child to adult. The key stages in this process are clearly indicated. Stephen actually develops in two parallel ways during the novel. He starts out as the willing accomplice of Keith,

aware of his 'incomprehensible good fortune' (p. 16) in being chosen to be Keith's friend and content to let him be the leader. However, the events of the summer cause him to grow away from Keith, who is increasingly revealed as the more immature. The catalyst for this independence is the other strand of Stephen's development: through the intervention of Barbara, he takes his first faltering steps towards adolescence and away from childish make-believe games. He is aware that something has changed, and he associates it explicitly with Barbara by calling it 'Lamorna' (the name of her house): 'It has a name, this sweet disturbance. Its name is Lamorna' (p. 168).

The smoking of his first cigarette, with a girl, is the symbol of the transition:

> I have a sense of freedom, as if I'm no longer bound by the rules and restric-
> tions of childhood. I can open locked boxes and break meaningless oaths with
> impunity. I'm on the verge of understanding mysteries that have been closed to
> me. I'm emerging from the old dark world of tunnels and terrors, and coming
> to a broad upland where the air's bright, and remote blue horizons open all
> around. (pp. 166–67)

He continues: 'Simple spying was part of the world of secret passages and bayonets that has just curled away with the blue smoke of the cigarette, and dispersed in the open sky' (pp. 167–68).

The process, once started, is accelerated by events. 'Once again I feel the locked box beginning to open and reveal its mysteries. I'm leaving behind the old tunnels and terrors of childhood — and stepping into a new world of even darker tunnels and more elusive terrors' (p. 180), he says when Mrs Hayward confides in him.

An indication of the change is Stephen's attitude to Keith's prohibitions and rules: 'I can open locked boxes and break meaningless oaths with impunity', he says (p. 167). Although Keith does carry out his threat to slit Stephen's throat, this is simply proof of his physical violence and no longer carries any moral authority.

Arguably, the process is completed in the confrontation between Stephen and Uncle Peter in the basement in the Barns. Although Peter is describing his breakdown as a pilot, the parallels with Stephen's situation are clear enough: 'You start playing some game, and you're the brave one, you're the great hero. But the game goes on and on, and it gets more and more frightening' (p. 203). This revelation destroys Stephen's childlike faith in heroes and heroism, as well as pointing out the real consequences of their childish game.

Note that, as is typical of children at this stage of their lives, Stephen reverts to more childish ways from time to time, for example on p. 192 when, unable to sleep, he creeps into his parents' bedroom and gets into their bed: 'I get on to the bottom of the bed and cautiously work my way up until I can edge myself under the covers and insinuate myself into the narrow canyon between their backs. I've become a child again.'

Spies

The title of a novel is always an important starting point for unravelling the author's intentions. The title is likely to be ambiguous, or resonant, or evocative in some way. Espionage is, of course, especially dangerous and feared in wartime, and during the Second World War there was something of an obsession with finding and unmasking enemy spies.

We can speculate upon why Frayn chose to call the novel *Spies*. The act of spying on Keith's mother is arguably what sets in train the novel's tragic events, although it could also be argued that the spying is merely voyeuristic and the source of the tragedy should be sought in the actions and omissions of the adults. The boys play at being spies, and end up observing something they had not anticipated. The fact that Stephen's father is finally revealed to have actually been involved in espionage (as a decrypt analyst, albeit *against* the Germans) seems at first sight like a mere plot device, but can finally be seen as an essential aspect of Stephen's status as an outsider in his own Close. The spy, also, is **archetypally** an alien, an outsider looking in. The *Boys' Own* type comics of the period frequently included stories in which plucky English boys unmasked **stereotypical** spies, and this may have coloured the attitudes of the boys.

A number of people can be accused of, or can be considered to be, spying on someone or something in the novel:

- Keith and Stephen spy on Mrs Hayward, initially, and then on the old 'tramp' who turns out to be Uncle Peter.
- Barbara Berrill spies on everything that happens in the Close as an exercise in power.
- Mrs Hayward spies on the boys who are watching her, out of a mixture of guilt and fear that she will be exposed.
- Mr Hayward, when his suspicions are aroused, spies on his wife to discover what she is up to.
- Uncle Peter (in the guise of the 'tramp') is described as a 'peeping tom' and is accused of spying on the inhabitants of the Close.
- Stephen's father actually is a spy, working on behalf of the British government.
- It is also possible to argue that in a small community such as the Close (note how the name reflects the close, introverted nature of the place), everybody spies on everybody else all the time.
- Old Stephen could be said to be spying on his former life, and acts as if he is spying on the current occupants of the Close as he walks up and down and peers at and into their houses.
- Finally, it can be argued that readers are made to spy on the characters and events of the Second World War story, and that, like a spy, they are given incomplete and at times contradictory information from which they must attempt to piece together a coherent story.

At the heart of the novel is the suggestion, raised by Keith at the outset, that his mother is a German spy. Curiously, this is never explored or explained. It is an important (but unanswered) question whether either or both of the boys ever actually 'believed' this suggestion. We are told that Keith was constantly conceiving of 'grand projects', for example 'a man-carrying glider' (p. 18) or a 'great intercontinental railway' (p. 19). We have no idea whether anything triggered Keith's claim that his mother was a spy, or whether it was an unrecognised hostility towards her, or just a mad idea. Perhaps he just wanted to impress Stephen.

Stephen never dared to argue with Keith, so he went along with it, and initially it was just a kind of detective game. Later, when it becomes clear that Mrs Hayward is concealing a real secret life, Stephen begins to become uneasy. He seems to have been a permanent victim of 'double-think', so that he both knew and did not know that the 'tramp' was Uncle Peter, and he both knew and did not know that Mrs Hayward was not really a German spy. This, of course, is the essence of children's make-believe games, which is what Mrs Hayward immediately recognised it as; but when it touches upon adult reality it becomes more important if the children forget that it is fantasy.

There is no evidence that Keith ever did realise that the spying make-believe, or anything else, was not reality; in fact, as the only child of (at least one) elderly parent(s), he seems to be disturbingly dissociated from reality. The scene in which he slits Stephen's throat is evidence that he is in reality a nasty, power-obsessed and immature creature, very like his father, whose idiom he borrows at this point. It is possible that Keith's denunciation of his mother reflects an unconscious siding with the father with whom he identifies; perhaps Mr Hayward already suspects or doubts her, and perhaps Keith has picked this up in some way.

It is over key questions such as this that the reader may feel frustrated by the mode of narration employed by the author. The present-day narrator knows perfectly well what was going on; but in attempting to reconstruct the state of mind of the young Stephen, it seems that he may be going too far in denying the young Stephen any real understanding of what is actually happening around him.

Equally central to the plot is the story of Uncle Peter, for this is what the boys' spying discovers (even though it is not at all what they had anticipated). The reader has to reconstruct Uncle Peter's story from a series of clues given at different times and in different ways. His own account on pp. 203–04 gives a fair indication of how it happened: he suffered a breakdown in the air on a mission: 'They trusted you and you failed them' (p. 203). But how long ago was this? Mrs Hayward admits that originally 'I used to look after Milly while Dee went' (p. 180), suggesting that it has been going on for some time (certainly before the boys started spying). Why did it change? Why did Mrs Hayward take over the duty? Was it because of the rumours, because originally Peter came to the railway bridge or even to the Close at night to see her, and was seen? Or was it because Mrs Hayward wanted to take the opportunity to rekindle her feelings for Peter? And did anything go on between them when she went to the Barns to see him? Was she even aware, consciously, that she was always Peter's first choice, even when he was marrying Dee?

The principal results of the interference of the boys are that, first, the croquet box is removed when Peter realises it has been discovered; this requires Mrs Hayward to go all the way to deliver things to him. Nevertheless, what really catches her out is her husband missing the thermos flask, which is nothing to do with the boys. When the boys discover the hiding place and thump on the roof, it must have been terrifying for those below, and they perhaps concluded then that the game was up, because the boys would be bound to betray them (in fact, the boys had no such intention and did not do so). They never actually had any idea what to do if they found a German spy, because it was only ever a game. Peter's deteriorating health, the fear of shame for Dee and the lack of any other way out seem to have been responsible for his final decision and fate, which it is hardly fair to blame on the boys. The adult situation was made by the adults, in all its complexity, and it is the failure of the adults to resolve it that leads to the tragedy.

Spying is inevitably corrosive of relationships because it requires both prying into the affairs of others and concealment. It also implies a lack of trust. The boys set out to spy on Mrs Hayward as one of Keith's childish 'projects'. No doubt she would have viewed it with the same indulgence with which she viewed the boys' other projects had it not been that she had a secret life that she wished to conceal. This was not, of course, the fault of the boys, nor did they know of it (although it remains an unresolved mystery what, if anything, led Keith to utter the six fatal words). What is clear is that their spying, unwittingly, forced Mrs Hayward's secret life into the open, causing a major rift between her and her husband, as well as, ultimately, one between Stephen and Keith. Whether it can be considered to have contributed to Uncle Peter's final breakdown is hard to assess; indeed, it is hard to see how the story could have had a happy ending, given his state of health and unwillingness to endure the humiliation of appearing in public and admitting to his breakdown.

For the boys it is just another game, and they are remarkably amateur at it; Mrs Hayward quickly becomes aware of it, and tries gently to shame Stephen out of continuing: 'That's what you're up to in here, is it? Keeping watch on us all, and writing it all down in your logbook?' (p. 107). (Note that she clearly does not think she can approach Keith.) 'For instance, I think it might be perhaps just a *tiny* bit rude if you actually followed people around' (p. 107). She makes valiant efforts to persuade him, but 'Her examples are unconvincing' (p. 109). Nevertheless, she is being very frank when she says 'Sometimes people have things they want to do in private…They have things they don't want everyone talking about' (p. 108). Later, she makes the key statement:

> When you and Keith started your little game of detectives…when you began looking in my things and following me around, I don't suppose it ever occurred to you that it would all end up like this, with me crying on your shoulder. Poor Stephen! It was a naughty thing to do, you know, spying on people. (p. 180)

What their spying has done is to force her to treat Stephen as a relative adult, appealing to his upbringing. It is curious, given all the other forms of middle-class manners, which have been drummed into Stephen, that he does not seem to feel that what they are doing is invading the privacy of adults; perhaps he feels that they are fair game. Stephen does recognise the consequences of his actions, however: 'And it's all my fault... Just by looking at things I shouldn't have looked at, I've changed them. I've set Keith's mother and father against each other. I've set Keith's mother and Auntie Dee against each other. I've ruined everything' (p. 179).

The wartime setting adds resonance to the novel in a number of ways. The events of the novel could not have happened, in the sense in which we have them, except in wartime; even if Peter had been an RAF pilot who had lost his nerve, he would simply have received psychiatric support. In wartime, and especially in view of his status as a 'hero', it would have led to insupportable humiliation for him and his family (even in the Second World War, post-traumatic stress disorder was little understood). Equally, wartime tends to be marked by an obsession with spies and espionage; and although spies were of equal importance after the war, there was no information of relevance that a housewife in suburban Ewell could have acquired. During the Second World War it was not mere schoolboy fantasy that details of aircraft being transported on the railway at the end of Mrs Hayward's garden would have been of military importance. Equally, Stephen's family would not have moved to England at all without the triumph of Nazism in Germany, which led inexorably to war, nor would his German origins have needed to remain secret.

However, the relationship between Stephen and Keith would have been the same in peacetime, as would the intervention of Barbara Berrill, and even without the trauma of Uncle Peter's death Stephen would presumably have grown up and drifted apart from Keith in due course.

Social background and the Close

Spies is set in a very specific milieu. Michael Frayn grew up in Ewell, Surrey, during the Second World War, and has stated that the novel is in part autobiographical. It is a novel with a remarkably limited immediate range: all the significant characters live in a tiny close of just 14 houses, a recently built housing development. Throughout the 1930s London was expanding rapidly, and was swallowing up towns and villages that had previously been some way distant from it, such as Uxbridge, Croydon, Kingston and Ewell. Often the expansion took the form of 'ribbon development' along the line of the railway, as is the case in the novel, where the Close backs on to the Southern Railway embankment, which plays such a prominent part in events.

There was a housing boom in the London suburbs between the wars, and 1930s semi-detached houses ('semis'), with their distinctive architecture, remain a prominent feature of these suburbs. 'The Close' is an example of such a recent development (see Chapter 5), and when the boys go under the railway bridge to the Lanes they are visiting an old country area typical of the area prior to the recent expansion. Indeed, when they go as far as the Barns, they are nearly at the next development, which, had it not been paused for 'the Duration' of the war, would have already met up with the Close.

The Close is a group of 14 middle-class houses of moderate size, standing in their own gardens. Numbers 2 and 3 are semi-detached, but all the others are detached houses. Given that the prevailing pattern of construction in the London suburbs in the 1930s was rows of semi-detached houses, this makes them relatively prestigious dwellings. The semi-detached ones were, of course, less so. Stephen shared a bedroom with Geoff, so theirs probably had either two bedrooms, or three with the third as a tiny 'box-room'; presumably the detached ones were larger. A further subtle distinction may be drawn between the houses with names and those merely numbered.

We learn a certain amount about the social status and occupation of most of the inhabitants of the Close:

- **The Wheatleys**. Mr Wheatley seems to have quite a responsible occupation, although we do not discover what it is until the end of the book; he is always travelling on government business. Nevertheless, it is quite clear that Stephen, young and old, is aware of his social inferiority to the Haywards; he shares a bedroom with his elder brother, and he goes to the wrong (but still independent) school.
- **The Haywards**. We never discover what occupation Mr Hayward has (or had, as he is probably retired. This is never stated). His wife is, of course, a middle-class housewife — a full-time occupation at that time, even though her only child is at least 12 years old. There are many indicators of middle-class status in the Hayward household (pp. 15–23).
- **The Berrills**. It is not clear whether Stephen views the Berrills as inferiors because of their social position or because they are girls. All we know is that their father is in the army — but we do not know whether he is an officer or an enlisted soldier.
- **Auntie Dee (Mrs Tracey)**. Auntie Dee has high status for two reasons: by reason of being Mrs Hayward's sister, and by virtue of being married to Peter, the RAF officer and hero.
- **The other inhabitants**. We know little about any of the other adults in the Close, but what we do know supports the view that most of them seem superficially to share similar conventional middle-class values: Mr Sheldon is forever clipping his hedge, the Hardiment children practise their scales on the piano, Mr McAfee is a special constable at the weekends but we do not know what his real job is. The Pinchers, though, the occupants of the other half of the Wheatleys' semi-detached house, are 'the undesirable elements in the Close' (p. 12) — partly because their garden 'was a dump for abandoned furniture warped by the rain, and offcuts of lumber and metal that Mr Pincher had stolen from work' (p. 12). They are characterised both by their relative poverty, in being unable to afford a detached house like the other residents

Plan of the Close and surrounding areas

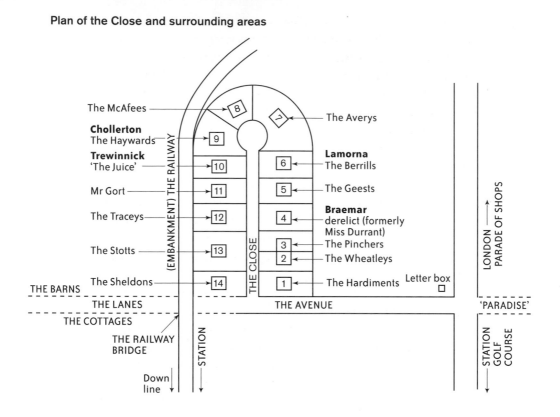

of the Close, and by their failure to keep the property in the tidy, house-proud way expected ('cleanliness is next to Godliness', as the proverb goes).

Stephen is acutely aware of his perceived inferiority to the Haywards, although he is less precise about its causes. 'We're socially colour-coded for ease of reference', he says (p. 15). 'The Haywards were impeccable' (p. 23), he summarises. Much of this impression derives from their house; note the words used when it is first described on p. 14: 'well-oiled', 'neat', 'heavy', 'solidity'. Once inside, the description is a eulogy of its solid, middle-class character, including the 'polished oak hallstand', 'dark oak panelling', 'matching watercolours', 'china plates', 'a grandmother clock' (p. 15). Later, the descriptions of the silver in the living room, and of Mr Hayward's garage, are all imbued with awe. The phrase 'irreproachably elegant lives' (p. 20) is actually attached to Mr Hayward's chickens, but might equally well be used of the Haywards themselves.

Keith goes to 'the right local preparatory school' (p. 16), whereas Stephen goes to the wrong one. Note that he does not seem aware that there were children not fortunate enough to go to private school at all; we are talking about subtle gradations within the highly stratified English middle class. Representatives of the lower classes, as epitomised by the sullen children living in the hovels in the lanes, are an incomprehensibly alien and irrelevant species.

Apart from the size, quality and furnishings of their respective homes, there is little objective difference between the two boys, except that Stephen accepts that Keith is the leader and he is the follower. The failure of Stephen's father to maintain the garden, though, is another sign of their inferiority: 'the promiscuous muddle of unidentified shrubs that my father never tended' (p. 11).

The issue was probably more acute for the parents. At various points it is possible to infer the middle-class habits that had been instilled in Stephen, especially the terror of 'germs' (now confused with 'Germans').

Social class was of immense importance in mid-twentieth-century Britain. It was especially of concern to those whose position in the all-important middle class was not secure. A professional occupation, or a large house, was sufficient evidence, but for those who could not demonstrate either, the crucial criterion was behaviour, which is why appearances and conformity to middle-class values and norms were considered so important. The Haywards illustrate a number of these norms; so do Stephen and his family, at least by implication:

- **Cleanliness and tidiness**. The Haywards' house was always immaculate, whereas Stephen's was not (and his bedroom was chaotic, while Keith's was always tidy). The Pinchers, though, with their cluttered garden, were even further down the scale.
- **Germs**. Stephen has had it drummed into him (to an almost comical extent) that he must avoid 'germs', and they are mentioned several times. When Barbara kisses him, 'I hadn't really got round to thinking about whether it was nice or not. I was too busy thinking about the germs' (p. 186). This partly reflects the recent advances in understanding the role germs play in causing infection; they were recognised as invaders of the body (just as Germans were invaders of the nation).
- **Proper speech**. Stephen has been taught to refer to adults with respect. This leads him to the comical situation on p. 148 where he is unable to refer to Keith's father in speaking to Mrs Hayward because he cannot find an appropriate way to refer to him!
- **Other indicators**. Speaking of Elizabeth Hardiment, Stephen says: 'her words carry authority because she wears glasses' (p. 159).

Middle-class virtues were defined as those that avoided the alleged viciousness, selfishness, criminality, filth and ignorance of the working classes. Working-class people were thought to be entirely at the mercy of low appetites, so middle-class people were required to show moderation and self-control in all things; they would never become drunk, or swear or be impolite, or behave indecorously. Routine, ritual and discipline were the middle-class virtues to be set against the working-class vices. The impoverished beings the boys passed on the way to the

Barns were an awful threat of the fate that awaited those who fell from the middle class. So, in his way, is Uncle Peter, because by failing to behave as a hero he has fallen to the lowest level of society and become an outcast.

Themes

There are many themes in *Spies* in addition to those already explored.

Homesickness/nostalgia

This theme pervades the book, but is brought into sharp focus by the retrospective final chapter. It permeates the entire novel because of the framing story, which sets it up from the start. 'Everything in the Close is as it was; and everything has changed' is the opening statement of the final chapter. The elder Stephen is deliberately revisiting the scene of his childhood trauma (which we assume he has not seen since he was a young man), for the express purpose (what other could there be?) of nostalgically immersing himself in the past. He goes into great detail at several points about how much has changed in the Close and the surrounding area since his childhood.

This nostalgia is made more telling when he reveals in the final chapter that the very concept of 'home' is, for him, a complex one. He does not identify the 'great German city' where he was born, but the Siemens company for which he worked was based in Berlin (one suburb is named 'Siemensstadt') and that would certainly fit with his father's sister having been bombed by 'Uncle Peter, or by his colleagues in Bomber Command' (p. 229). He explains about the concepts of *Fernweh* and *Heimweh* (p. 229, rather unclearly), explicitly drawing attention to the idea of a yearning for home.

Memory

This is obviously a central theme of the novel. As early as p. 31, Frayn draws attention to this key theme by making old Stephen interrupt his story to say: 'No, wait. I've got that wrong.' This is a curious device; it suggests, implausibly, that old Stephen is actually 'telling' this story to a live audience — why else draw attention to such a mistake? Why not simply go back and write the correct version? The answer, surely, is to draw attention to memory as a concept and theme, and to its limitations and fallibility. This is part of Frayn's attempt to undermine the idea of a simple 'story' that is being told to the reader. Even when he is telling the story through the **persona** of young Stephen, this does not necessarily mean that what is recounted is reliable. Not only does it (generally) reflect what Stephen knew or did not know at that time; it is actually old Stephen's unreliable memory of those events more than 50 years later.

Nevertheless, memory is what the novel is all about. Old Stephen has been reminded, by the distinctive smell of privet (note that smell is the strongest sense), and has returned to his past, both physically and mentally, in order to relive those life-changing events from so long ago. And even if his memory may be shaky about some of the details (in particular, the order in which things happened) he is in no doubt about the emotional truth of what happened. Frayn sums up: 'It's so difficult to remember what order things occurred in — but if you can't remember *that*, then it's impossible to work out which led to which, and what the connection was' (p. 32).

Women and love

A number of female characters play important roles in helping Stephen to gain an understanding of the opposite sex and relationships with them as he begins the journey from child to young adult during this eventful summer. He is particularly influenced by two contrasting females: Barbara Berrill and Mrs Hayward. Barbara Berrill forces her way into his life, overcoming his reluctance and lack of interest by a mixture of bullying, cajoling and superior knowledge and experience. She forces the pace, making him grow up, and although Stephen is very much the follower in this (as in pretty much everything else), he does not object to where she is leading him. They get as far as smoking together and having a couple of rather wooden kisses before events take over and Barbara's interest wanes.

It is Mrs Hayward who is arguably even more important in helping Stephen to grow out of his childish dependence and self-centredness. Stephen's admiration for Mrs Hayward may be tinged with an appreciation of her beauty, as well as her composure and elegance. It is evident that he does not know how to deal with her: 'Where do you look, for a start, when there's nowhere to look except at her?' (p. 105). Initially he sees her as an aloof goddess, and as late as p. 175 he can still describe her as 'somehow even more perfect than before'. His view of her is so idealised that there is a suggestion that he may be attracted to her, or that he sees her as a perfect example of womanhood. But he is forced to develop his understanding as circumstances throw them together, and reveal the older woman as vulnerable and in need of his assistance and understanding: 'I feel pained that she's had to humiliate herself before me in this way' (p. 110). Finally, Uncle Peter's revelation that he has always really loved Mrs Hayward, although he married Dee, gives Stephen a glimpse of the complexity of adult relationships.

Interestingly, these two key characters become conflated at the climax of the novel. As Keith is cutting Stephen's throat, Stephen ponders the ambiguity of his statement 'You showed her our things' (p. 209), particularly as both Barbara and Mrs Hayward have visited the hideout more than once: 'I have the odd idea that in some strange way we're talking about both of them' (p. 211).

There are other women in the novel who play subsidiary roles:

- Stephen's elder brother, Geoff, has in fact already trodden the path Barbara is offering Stephen with her elder sister, Deirdre; but whereas Barbara has clearly taken a keen interest in this, it is indicative of Stephen's non-relationship with his brother, or his absolute lack of interest in the topic, that he knows nothing about it.
- Auntie Dee is another example of wifely love, but we very rarely see her at first hand and are unable to judge the quality of her relationship with Uncle Peter, except that she basks in the reflected glory of his heroic reputation. In particular, we do not know whether she is aware of the complicated relationship between her sister and her husband.
- Stephen's mother is quietly loyal to and supportive of her husband (but then, we discover, they have been through extraordinary experiences together). She is not very demonstrative or passionate, or at least not that Stephen notices.

Family life

We are presented with two very different families in the novel, the Haywards and the Wheatleys. Curiously, we learn less about the Wheatleys as a family than we do about the Haywards, because neither young nor old Stephen says much about the Wheatleys until the final chapter. We scarcely see the relationship between Mr and Mrs Wheatley at all. The age difference between Geoffrey and Stephen is big enough for the two brothers to have nothing in common, despite sharing a bedroom, and Geoffrey is barely a character in the novel. Although both parents are clearly concerned about Stephen, his repeated refusal to tell them anything means that they have to guess what is going on in his world. This is not the result of fear: Stephen is not afraid of punishment in the way that Keith, rightly, is. Rather, it is the result of his confusion over the ambiguities of what he is doing, and the conflicts between the different values he is trying to juggle — duty to adults, promises to Keith, the need for secrecy. Note that he is still able, when sufficiently distressed, to creep into their bed and sleep between them (p. 192) — which could be seen as an image of a loving and protecting family, or alternatively as an indication that Stephen has not yet grown up.

The Haywards, by contrast, are a worrying family. Mr Hayward is repressed and authoritarian. Mrs Hayward is too good to be true, but behind her elegance and composure she turns out to be acting more deceitfully than any other character in the novel. Keith is a strange boy, an only child who is both more and less mature than his years in various ways. As the novel proceeds he gravitates more and more closely to his father, despite the tension and suppressed violence in their relationship (Mr Hayward beats him on p. 146), and increasingly adopts his father's clipped idiom as the outward sign of this. There is no evidence of any warmth between the two adults, and little if any communication (although the occasional exclamation marks in the diary suggest that they still sleep together from time to time).

Mrs Hayward seems to grow apart from Keith, too, during the course of the novel, symbolised by the times she seeks Stephen out and confides in him. It is hard to imagine that she confides in Keith in any way. When we discover, shockingly, that the Hayward penchant for slitting throats has been tried out on her before being inflicted on Stephen (p. 211), it is not clear whether it was father, or son, or both, who actually performed the act of punishment: 'I suddenly realise where he learnt to practise this particular form of torture with this particular instrument, and why his mother, in the heat of summer, has taken to wearing that cravat pinned high around her neck.' One can only surmise the kind of atmosphere inside a house where such acts can be perpetrated. Mrs Hayward is undoubtedly also terrified of her husband's cold anger, because she not only submits to the punishment, but accepts his order not to go to see Dee any more. No wonder she was forced to resort to subterfuge and deception in order to go to see Peter; no wonder, either, that she found him more attractive than her husband. Whether she actually had a physical relationship with Peter, however, is left to the reader to speculate.

England and Germany

Frayn has a considerable interest in Germany; in addition to *Spies*, two of his recent plays (*Copenhagen* and *Democracy*) are set there.

The whole novel is a testament to a character whose loyalties, and whose concept of home, are divided between England and Germany. At the end we understand the circumstances that brought this about (although we are given no indication as to how Stephen's English, and presumably non-Jewish, mother came to be married to a German in the early 1930s).

But this is not quite enough. Stephen had no memory of the 'quiet, garden-lined street' (p. 229) in which he spent his first two years, and yet he felt sufficiently unsettled to move himself back to his 'rediscovered homeland' (p. 229) in early middle age. Once there, he felt that each of his homelands was a 'dreamlike echo' (p.229) of the other. The physical similarity of the two streets, his ability to feel both at home, and yet not wholly at home, in both, is perhaps the strongest indication of a fundamental link between the two cultures, all the more **ironic** in view of the complicated web of loyalties in Stephen's family history. His father had fled Germany, where he was being persecuted, and then worked actively against its regime during the war (thereby identifying himself with Germany's enemy and contributing to its defeat). Stephen, brought up as English, saw the Germans as enemies (which they, or at least the Nazis, doubly were), and saw what they had done to his neighbourhood (bombing 'Braemar', killing Miss Durrant) and to Uncle Peter. Nevertheless, he concluded

that Germany was his spiritual home and made the difficult transition to live there. Yet when he returned to the Close, so many years later, that also felt like a homecoming.

Perception/appearance and reality

At the centre of the novel is a series of perceptions and misperceptions by various characters, but principally by Stephen. There are a number of gaps between appearance and reality. The seemingly perfect relationship of Mr and Mrs Hayward turns out to be a sham. Mrs Hayward, the perfect middle-class housewife, is engaged in a pattern of deceptive behaviour to hide what she is really doing, and lives in constant fear of being discovered. Keith, apparently the perfect schoolboy, is an immature and vicious bully. Stephen, apparently meek, ends up betraying almost everybody at one point or another, because he is unable to fix his loyalties securely in the face of the complex relationships he is involved in.

Everyone initially underestimates what everyone else is capable of: Stephen and Keith are capable of systematically spying on Keith's mother; Mrs Hayward is capable of living an extended lie; Keith is capable of inflicting actual pain on Stephen; Barbara is capable of cynically manipulating Stephen for her own ends; and Stephen's father is leading a double life.

Stephen and the whole of his family are, of course, not what they seem. Nor is Uncle Peter, or, to look at it another way, nor is the German spy/tramp in the Barns.

There is also an issue about the way perceptions are presented by the novelist. Young Stephen is a child, and much of the novel is narrated through his eyes. Old Stephen knows a great deal more (with the benefit of hindsight), but mischievously conceals his adult perceptions for most of the book; he also subverts this concealment, however, by giving authorial comments and hints about what was really going on. Stephen's perceptions are naive and are frequently coloured by his preconceptions: of Auntie Dee, he ironically comments 'No one could smile like that and have any secrets from the world' (p. 103).

Secret knowledge

A key corollary of secrecy and duplicity is secret knowledge. Auntie Dee and Mrs Hayward both secretly know what has happened to Uncle Peter, but they know that they must not divulge this or he will be shamed, and Dee and her sister will also be shamed by association. Stephen gains secret knowledge of who the tramp is, but also understands that it is essential to maintain secrecy: 'Whatever I secretly knew, and whenever I knew it, I also understood that it was something that must never be known' (p. 234). Both of Stephen's parents have the secret knowledge of their own background, and of Stephen's father's role in the British war effort, but they succeed in concealing this so thoroughly that their own children have no inkling of it. All of these are deadly serious parallels to the childish secrets that Keith attempts to keep, and also to Barbara's desperate attempts to secure access to real secrets by trading trivial and childish ones.

The other great secret of the novel is, of course, the truth about Stephen's origins. Even though no hint is given of the German connection, there are sufficient suggestions of the possibility of Jewishness for the perceptive reader to presume that this is the case: the reference to 'cabbalistic' on p. 63, to Stephen being called a 'sheeny' on p. 64 (and his father's reaction to it), and the hints at sensitivity to Friday evening (a holy time for Jews): 'why there's something awkward about going out to play on Friday evenings' (p. 64).

Duty/heroism

Duty is a particularly powerful concept in times of war. All middle-class children were brought up with a strong sense of duty, and Stephen Wheatley is no exception. Whenever an adult speaks firmly to him, he knows it is his duty to obey, whether it is his own father, or Keith's father, or Uncle Peter. Stephen, however, is aware of the conflict that may be involved, particularly when Mr Hayward orders him to hand over the basket, which he knows will incriminate Mrs Hayward. What Uncle Peter says when Stephen finally confronts him is important because it subverts the simplistic concept of duty that Stephen has been taught: 'You start playing some game, and you're the brave one, you're the great hero…you can't go on being brave for ever' (p. 203). But Stephen is 'still helplessly obedient to adult authority' (p. 201) and feels 'There's nothing for it but to obey' (p. 204). Note that heroism and duty are particularly middle-class values; Stephen refers to 'the silver-framed heroes on the altars in the Haywards' house' (p. 130) as the starting point for his 'journey from the highest to the lowest' (p. 130) when he visits the Barns.

There is an additional **irony** about the concept of Uncle Peter being a 'hero'. Although it was rare for anyone to question such concepts explicitly at the time, we now have a more ambivalent attitude: although the dangers involved in being a bomber pilot were real enough, what Peter and his colleagues were actually doing was bombing and killing (mostly) defenceless civilians. The policy of 'area bombing' made no attempt to discriminate between legitimate military targets and others; hospitals, schools, women and children were all bombed. Those on the receiving end described such bombing as barbaric, whichever side was doing it. How 'heroic' would we view such behaviour as being today? There may be at least an implicit criticism by Frayn of Stephen's unthinking acceptance of 'duty'.

Loyalty and betrayal

Stephen, as a dedicated follower, gives unthinking loyalty to his leader. For most of the novel this is Keith, and Stephen does not dare question Keith's position or leadership, even when he is aware of failings, for example the frequent mis-spellings ('Secrit', 'Privet'). He does not seem to have the capacity to question those in

positions of authority, i.e. all adults, or those to whom he accords such a position (Keith, and to a degree Barbara). By showing loyalty to one, however, he is required to show disloyalty to another, and Stephen finds this dilemma difficult (and generally avoids it, where possible, by remaining silent).

Stephen believes that he betrays everybody at some point or other in the novel. He certainly betrays his oath to Keith 'Never to reveal anything about all this to anyone' (p. 55) by allowing Barbara to open the trunk, and also arguably by tacitly allowing Mrs Hayward to discover what they have secretly been doing. He betrays Mrs Hayward by allowing Mr Hayward to take the basket. You could claim that he never actually betrays Uncle Peter, although the violent attack on his hiding place makes matters worse for him.

Mrs Hayward also shows loyalty, both to her sister Dee and to Uncle Peter, which of course involves her being disloyal to her own husband. You could argue that she shows disloyalty also to her own son when she decides to ask Stephen to take the basket to the Barns, not Keith. Mrs Hayward's motives for the deceptions that she practises are, of course, dubious if she acknowledges the attraction between Uncle Peter and her. Surely, the loyalty she owes to her husband should require her to inform him of the true situation with Uncle Peter?

Mrs Hayward is clearly betraying her husband by concealing her secret visits from him, and probably is betraying him emotionally as well by her feelings for Peter, whether consummated or not. She is presumably also betraying her sister by allowing herself to become emotionally entangled with Dee's husband under the guise of helping him. (Does Dee know or suspect this? We are given no indication.)

Uncle Peter believes he has betrayed his country by failing in his patriotic duty to be a hero. No one, though, is betraying their country by being a spy for the enemy, except for Stephen's father, and even he would no doubt claim he was being loyal to the 'true' Germany by fighting against the Nazis who had taken Germany over and subverted its character.

Fall from grace

Some critics have seen a Christian aspect to *Spies*. Uncle Peter is initially presented in hagiographical terms, i.e. as if he were a saint; 'the glory of Uncle Peter' on p. 25, and the use of 'altars' on p. 130; and he typifies the biblical idea of the fall from grace, seen in the story of Adam and Eve. He is worshipped as a hero, although not on an individual level; Stephen is quite clear that it is the uniform, the 'three famous initials' (p. 25), which define his heroism. There is no claim that he actually performed any individually heroic actions. And his fall from this elevated station is as complete as it could be. To emphasise this, Stephen twice uses the metaphor of the fall in a way almost reminiscent of Dante: on p. 130, the 'journey from the highest to the lowest', and again on p. 196, describing Mrs Hayward as 'descending the great ladder of the world, rung by rung'. Peter has become an outcast, beneath contempt, having failed both in his class duty and his patriotic duty, and he has sufficiently assimilated the values that dominate this society to know that he has no alternative but to put an end to himself, above all to avoid the 'shame' that would descend on Auntie Dee and young Milly if his disgrace were to become known.

There are other references to religion. The use of the word 'disciple' in describing Stephen's relationship with Keith suggests a perception of a messianic character, which is not supported by the evidence, but which perhaps reflects the nature of Stephen's subservience: 'I see now that he was only the first in a whole series of dominant figures in my life whose disciple I became' (p. 16). The bayonet in the trunk, 'our most secret and sacred possession' (p. 55), is directly compared to the Christian host: 'It both is and is not the sacred bayonet, just as the wafer and the wine both are and are not the body and blood of a being who both is and is not a god' (p. 55). Frayn makes the tongue-in-cheek comparison on p. 25: 'The ways of the Haywards were no more open to questioning or comprehension than the domestic arrangements of the Holy Family.'

Town and country

At the beginning of Chapter 5, old Stephen emphasises how new the development was of which the Close formed part. Until just a few years earlier, this had all been countryside. The Close is an **archetype** of a controlled, manageable, unthreatening environment; self-contained, with just 14 houses and only one entrance, it is like a womb. Even emerging onto the nearby streets seems like an expulsion from the Garden of Eden. The unconquered countryside areas neighbouring this new suburb are described in a variety of terms, but they all have in common fear, and a fall from suburban grace into an old and threatening world: 'the last pocket of the rural world pursued its ancient, secret life. Each of the rare excursions we made into it was a frightening adventure, a series of ordeals to test our coming manhood' (p. 89); or 'another, more ancient and frightening land' (p. 126), echoed in 'that skulking, ancient land beyond the tunnel' (p. 132). The inhabitants of these areas are alien and terrifying. Stephen's final journey to the Barns, in Chapter 9, is couched in terms of a journey to the underworld: 'once again I set out on that horrible journey' (p. 194), passing 'the disheartening landmarks' (p. 194); he summarises it as 'The living grave' (p. 195). Stephen sees Mrs Hayward as making the journey from her perfect middle-class existence to the underworld every time she comes to see Uncle Peter (p. 196):

> I think of Keith's mother, coming out of the world of silver ornaments and silver chimes and descending the great ladder of the world, rung by rung, until she finds herself where I'm standing, in the smell of the elders and the excrement — and then going on, further down, into the underworld.

War

The war has changed the lives of the inhabitants of the Close in a number of ways. There is the blackout, and the blackened ruins of Braemar are a constant reminder of the threat from above. Although rationing is not much referred to, it limited the ability to shop and to cook. 'Paradise', down the Avenue, is described as 'the tangle of mucky smallholdings where our neighbours went to buy unrationed eggs, or a rooster for Christmas' (p. 87). In addition to increased vigilance, the war has led Mr McAfee to become a special constable and Mr Hayward to return to the army as a reservist.

Living in a small community

Although the Close is part of a suburban town, it is sufficiently self-contained to constitute a closed community. Everybody is aware of everybody else's actions; it is virtually impossible to have secrets in such a community. There is constant gossip, and all the residents inevitably 'spy' on each other. Note the conversation that ensues when the police officer calls on Auntie Dee (pp. 158–62). All the children share rumours, gossip, and prejudices about the other inhabitants. It is against this background that Mrs Hayward's plea to Stephen should be seen: 'Sometimes people have things they want to do in private…They have things they don't want everyone talking about' (p. 108). This is particularly an issue in a middle-class community where everyone is attempting to 'keep up appearances' and conform in order to persuade doubters that they really are worthy of being considered 'middle-class'.

Images, symbols and motifs

Various images, symbols and motifs play recurring roles in the novel.

Lamorna

The long 'or' sound gives this word a melancholy and nostalgic tone. It is the name of Barbara Berrill's house and by **metonymy** it comes, for Stephen, to stand for all the feelings of the awakening of first love, and subsequent loss, associated with Barbara and, more generally, with that momentous coming-of-age summer. The house is named after a cove in Cornwall, which itself has romantic associations; there was a Lamorna Artists' Colony, set up in 1890 by S. J. 'Lamorna' Birch as a satellite of the Newlyn Artists' Colony. There was also a romantic folksong, about love and loss, named 'Lamorna' (see pp. 35–36 of this guide).

Privet

The smell of privet plays a pivotal role in the novel because it is this which first triggers old Stephen's nostalgia about his childhood in England. But it is not a neutral smell: 'It has a kind of sexual urgency to it' (p. 3), because it is a smell which only comes during the shrub's reproductive period, and is a sign of the 'coming of age' of the plant — just as it marks the same for Stephen. The smell is pungent and unpleasant. It comes in June, when the events of the novel occur. The privet also plays an important role as the place of concealment and observation from which the boys do the 'spying' of the title. It is also close to the word 'private' — another theme of the novel. Mrs Hayward begs for the right of adults to have some privacy, but spying denies this right. The connection is comically pointed out by Keith's ignorant mis-spelling of his attempt at a 'Private' notice for their hideout as 'privet'. It echoes one of the most famous stirrings of memory in literary history — at the beginning of Marcel Proust's great novel sequence *A la recherche du temps perdu*, the writer is reminded of the past by the taste of a *madeleine* (a kind of cake).

Cigarettes

Smoking cigarettes is seen by Stephen (young and old) as a key symbol, a rite of passage, because it happens with Barbara and is associated with throwing off his childish attachment to Keith and, tentatively (and, ultimately, unsuccessfully) replacing it with a relationship with Barbara: 'It tastes of importance and of being grown up' (p. 166). This was an association explicitly promoted by the advertising material of the time (before the link with cancer was known), and it was obviously effective in making smoking seem desirable to young people.

The railway

The railway is a key motif of the novel: it marks the limit of the boys' world, because it forms the boundary of the Close. All day, the trains emerge from the cutting travel over the embankment and vanish to the new station. It is a symbol of modern technology and the bringer of civilisation (without it this suburb would not have been built). It is a constant reminder of the war, because the goods trains frequently carry war materials, offering opportunities to German spies living adjacent to the line to find useful information to send to their masters. It also brings death to Uncle Peter, acting as a kind of *deus ex machina*; it is appropriate that the train that kills him is seen by Stephen to be carrying damaged RAF aircraft. New technology brings new benefits, but also new dangers: it is powered by electricity, and the exposed third rail is lethal to any creature stepping onto it (as Uncle Peter demonstrates). We are warned of this naked power early on in the novel: 'the showers of sparks they throw up from the live rail' (p. 31). It may be used (as aircraft were) for good or for waging war.

Language, style, structure and voice

Although *Spies* is written in a deceptively simple style, there is subtlety in the language, imagery and structure used.

Viewpoint and the two narrators

The novel is effectively told by two narrators, because old Stephen regularly adopts the voice of young Stephen. In this, as in much else, *Spies* is a curious hybrid. The novel is set in two distinct times — the present day and 50 years earlier — but the episodes are not clearly distinguishable. Similarly, there are not real multiple viewpoints, because the whole novel is narrated by the present-day Stephen, but at numerous points he adopts the **persona**, perspective and responses of the earlier Stephen (at least to an extent). These episodes are characterised by the change to third-person narration ('he' in place of 'I'), although it is still Stephen. This is, of course, a simple shorthand way for the present-day narrator to distance himself (but not *too* far) from his childhood self. This distance is frequently and tantalisingly pulled back (by the overt change of perspective to the present day) so that the reader is denied the satisfaction of being immersed in the Second World War narrative.

The use of tenses

The use of tenses is subtle and complicated, and achieves a number of effects. The following are the main tenses used:

(1) In the framing story, old Stephen writes in the *present tense* about his visit to the Close as it occurs, e.g. 'I stand on the corner' (p. 9), 'I walk to the corner of the Close' (p. 87).

(2) Also in the framing story, old Stephen sometimes writes in the *conventional past tense* about past events, e.g. 'From those six random words, anyway, came everything that followed' (p. 33).

(3) A *third-person historic present tense* (continuous commentary) is used to describe old Stephen's reconstruction of young Stephen's actions as if he is an observer across time: 'Stephen's already crossing over the road…He's walking slowly' (p. 13). This is unusual in referring to young Stephen in the third person.

(4) A *first-person historic present tense* is used when old Stephen in the framing story explicitly places himself in the position of young Stephen at the time: 'How do I react to the news? Do I offer any comment?' (p. 37). This should be a past, but by using the present he makes the dilemma immediate and current.

(5) A *first-person present tense* is used by young Stephen to tell his story as it happens, e.g. 'I look at the photographs in the silver frames' (p. 45).

(6) A *prospective tense* (an example of **prolepsis**) is employed when old Stephen, telling young Stephen's story, looks ahead to what is to come, e.g. 'What a surprise all the ordinary, dull citizens of the Close…are going to be getting very shortly!' (p. 44).

(7) A *composite tense* (a past tense embedded in a present-tense narrative, which is itself set in the past) is used when old Stephen is telling the story from the perspective of young Stephen but inserts an observation based upon an adult perspective, e.g. 'that part of a lady, as I've known for at least a year now, is her bosom' (p. 106).

The Postmodernist device

The structure of the novel is interesting. At first sight, there is a conventional framing story in the present day to begin and end the novel; and in between there is an earlier story, told by the narrator of the framing story in his childhood **persona**. He is looking nostalgically back to this story. This simple structure is, however, subverted by the author in two ways. First, he keeps pulling back from the Second World War story to offer comments by the framing narrator; this breaks the continuity and tension of the earlier story, although it also places it in perspective. Second, by interrupting the narration in this way, the author is able to avoid actually telling the climaxes of the Second World War story in their appropriate place. This is a characteristic Postmodernist device.

A number of readers are frustrated by what they view as the failings of *Spies*, and it has been suggested that this is the result of its Postmodernist character. Many readers report that, although they are gripped by the Second World War story, they feel frustrated by the way in which it is narrated, and in particular by a number of its features:

- the refusal of the author to either (a) let old Stephen tell the story with hindsight; or (b) let young Stephen tell the story, with all the limitations of his childish knowledge and understanding
- the implausibility of even a naive Stephen failing to appreciate the identity of Uncle Peter, even when he is speaking to him
- the refusal of the novelist to give the reader the satisfaction of a recognition scene, or of the tragic final scene

These are all characteristics of Postmodernist fiction. The goal of the Postmodernist author is to subvert the conventional fictional **genre**, where the reader expects to be told a 'story' from the perspective of an omniscient narrator who not only knows everything, but is also, as it were, 'honour-bound' to tell a complete and coherent story, probably keeping to the conventions of a particular genre (tragedy, **romance** etc).

Although Frayn does have a story to tell, he is trying to do a number of other things as well. He wishes to draw attention to the incomplete knowledge that the participants in events actually have, both at the time and, very often, in retrospect. He wishes to emphasise that nostalgic accounts of childhood are, in the real world, inherently unreliable; the memory plays tricks, changes the order of events, deletes details entirely and distorts the memory of perceptions, which may in any case have been false in the first place. There is, therefore, no simple, single 'story' that can be told; there is what Stephen thought and knew at the time, and there is what Stephen remembers, reconstructs and infers 50 years on. The young Stephen was clearly a confused and frightened child, easily led, reluctant to face up to the reality that surrounded him; he also clung stubbornly to ideas long after the objective evidence had undermined them.

A good example of this is his attitude to the suggestion that Keith's mother was a spy. When the suggestion was originally made, it is described as 'those six random words' (p. 33) — drawing attention to the arbitrary nature of causes and consequences. No evidence was ever provided for this assertion; Keith never said why this thought had occurred to him. Did even he ever believe it? This is hard to answer, because childhood games are entirely composed of such 'double-think': the boys knew perfectly well that there was no transcontinental railway in the garden, but nevertheless immersion in the pretence is a condition of playing the game. Once a child is too self-conscious to bury itself in such make-believe, the games become impossible and the child grows up. Stephen always seems to be aware that this is only a game; but it is a dangerous game, because it impacts closely upon real people and real life, especially in wartime. (If, of course, Mrs Hayward had had nothing to hide, the game would have fizzled out pretty quickly.) As it happened, the game of spying on Mrs Hayward as a 'spy' turned up evidence that she was engaged in a substantial and extended deception in real life; the game thus crossed the boundary (just as the novel crosses boundaries) between make-believe and reality. But the boys were not equipped to deal with this, especially as what they had stumbled upon by their 'spying' was dramatically different from what they had anticipated; their limited experience of life, coupled with their preconceptions, prevented them from recognising what they had found for what it really was. Stephen, always arguably less immersed in these games than Keith, was apparently at least partially conscious of this ambiguous reality: 'How did he and Keith's mother communicate? If she's a German spy she presumably speaks German... But she *isn't* a German spy! Is she? That all belongs to a past I've long since left behind. Haven't I?' (p. 194). (This is part of a section narrated by young Stephen in the present tense, but it sounds much more like old Stephen looking back.)

Similarly, Stephen is always subject to a comparable ambiguity about Uncle Peter: he has to be a German spy/tramp, therefore he cannot be Uncle Peter, who in any case is a 'hero', and therefore cannot be a tramp. To a degree Stephen is trammelled both by the conventional categories of his upbringing and by his own preconceptions. Nevertheless, Frayn's refusal to allow him ever to acknowledge the blindingly obvious, even when Peter calls him 'Stephen', refers to everyone else by name and is sitting opposite him, is taking this ambiguity to an extreme degree. Old Stephen acknowledges this in the final chapter (pp. 233–34):

> Did I really not know at the time that the broken man in the Barns was Uncle Peter? Of course I knew. I knew as soon as he called me by name. No, before that. As soon as I heard him behind me in the moonlight. Or much earlier still, even. From the very beginning, perhaps...I went on thinking, even after I'd heard him speak, that he was a *German*. This was what I clung on to — that he was a *German*...Whatever I secretly knew, and whenever I knew it, I also understood that it was something that must never be known.

The apparent weaknesses of the novel may therefore be seen to be evidence of a deeper novelistic purpose, which gives added depth and seriousness to a tale of an old man's nostalgia for the events of his childhood.

Irony

There are numerous instances of **irony** in the text, a device of which Frayn is particularly fond. The complexity of Stephen's relations with Germany and England give ample examples. That his father really was a German spy (but not a spy for Germany), while he was trying to prove that Mrs Hayward actually was one, is a clear irony (especially as she was helping Uncle Peter, who had suffered greatly in the war effort to destroy Germany). So is the fact that Uncle Peter, or one of his fellows, was responsible for killing Stephen's aunt and children, although as Jews they were victims of the Nazi regime, not supporters of it.

Further examples of irony include the following:

- When Stephen goes to the tramp in the Barns (p. 130), he describes his trip as 'a journey from the highest to the lowest — from the silver-framed heroes on the altars in the Haywards' house…to an old derelict taking refuge under a sheet of corrugated iron in a stinking elder bush'. The reader knows (although Stephen does not) that the same person is being described: Uncle Peter in the silver frame, and Uncle Peter the derelict.
- On numerous occasions there is the irony that the reader (and, of course, old Stephen) recognises and understands what the naive young Stephen does not, e.g. 'sheeny' and Jewishness on p. 64, or the marks in Mrs Hayward's diary.
- Stephen's naivety also leads to ironies: 'No one could smile like that and have any secrets from the world' (p. 103), he says of Auntie Dee, when in fact no one has more.

Word play

There are a number of occasions on which young Stephen reveals his ignorance or naivety by misunderstanding words, or inappropriately associating them with similar-sounding ones. Frayn cannot avoid playing with language, usually for humorous effect. Stephen is obsessed with germs, and cannot avoid linking Germans and germs in his mind; they pose an equal threat to his British way of life (e.g. 'germ-laden Germans', p. 141).

The game with the word 'privet' is even more elaborate; Keith's ignorant mis-spelling of the 'Private' sign in the privet hedge allows Barbara to be sarcastic and causes genuine humorous confusion on the part of Mrs Hayward when she visits. Stephen takes this a stage further (an extension of his obsession with germs, perhaps) when he links it with 'privy': 'I know perfectly well what privets are…lavatories of some sort, and of some particularly disgusting sort that's full of germs' (p. 97). Note that Frayn does not mention the word 'privy' at all, relying on the reader to understand the pun.

Another, less amusing, example is Stephen's assumption, when mentioning the word 'sheeny' has him brought before his father, that the offence is 'I'd heard the "she" in it, and grasped that it was some secret thing to do with girls' (p. 64).

Literary terms and concepts

Assessment Objective 1 requires 'insight appropriate to literary study, using appropriate terminology'; therefore a knowledge of literary terms is a necessity for A-level English Literature students. It has the further benefit of allowing responses to text to be precise and concise. The literary terms below, many of which will already be known from GCSE studies, are used in this book and are relevant to an understanding of the traditions and styles of the novel. You may wish to add examples from the text next to the relevant definitions.

archetype   original model or idea used as a recurrent symbol

cliché   predictable and overused expression or situation

closure   a sense of an ending, tying up the ends in a fictional work

contextuality   historical, social and cultural background of a text

deconstruct   analyse critically; break something up into its constituent parts

deus ex machina   sudden outside intervention in the plot of a play or novel to sort out a situation. It means literally a 'god from the machinery', i.e. above the stage, arriving to put things right at the end of a play

genre   type or form of writing

intertextuality   relationship between one text and another

irony   language intended to mean the opposite of the words actually expressed; or an amusing or cruel reversal of a situation which is expected, intended or deserved

lyrical   expression of strong feelings, usually love; suggestive of music

metonymy   substituting an attribute for the thing itself; for example, Lamorna (the name of a house) comes to represent Barbara and everything she stands for

persona   voice within a text acting as narrator

plurality   possible multiple meanings of a text

Postmodernism contemporary literary movement, beginning around 1950

prolepsis an anticipation of future events

romance popular story of love and war, deriving from medieval court life and fairy tale

self-reflexive term describing a work that calls explicit attention to how it has been constructed

stereotype typical characteristics of a category of person (e.g. British army officers), often used for mockery

Questions & Answers

LITERATURE

Essay questions, specimen plans and examiner notes

Exam essays

Refer to page 6 for a more detailed discussion of examination essay techniques. You need to know exactly which Assessment Objectives are being tested by your exam board and where the heaviest weighting falls. You will probably have looked at or practised questions from past papers so that you know what kind of title to expect, and it would be helpful if your teacher shared with you the examiners' reports for previous years' exams. Close reference to text is required even in closed-book examinations, and as quotation demonstrates 'use of text', it is often the most concise way of supporting a point. You are, however, more likely in a closed-book exam to be set a general question dealing with structural or generic issues, theme or characterisation, often based on a critical comment. Even in an open-book exam the best-performing students do not need to refer to their text very often, so do not be intimidated if you are sitting a closed-book exam.

Essay questions fall into the following categories: close section analysis and relation to whole text; characterisation; setting and atmosphere; sequence and structure; genre; language and style; themes and issues. Remember, however, that themes are relevant to all essays, and that analysis, not just description, is always required. Exam essays should be clearly structured, briskly argued, concisely expressed, closely focused, and supported by brief but constant textual references. They should show a combination of familiarity, understanding, analytical skill and informed personal response. Length is not in itself an issue — quality matters rather than quantity — but you have to prove your knowledge and fulfil the assessment criteria, and without sufficient coverage and exploration of the title you cannot be awarded a top mark. Aim realistically for approximately 12 paragraphs or four sides of A4.

Do not take up one absolute position and argue only one interpretation. There are no 'yes' or 'no' answers in literature. The other side must have something to be said for it or the question would not have been set, so consider both views before deciding which one to argue, and mention the other one first to prove your awareness of different reader opinions and reactions. It is permissible to say your response is equally balanced, provided that you have explained the contradictory evidence and have proved that ambivalence is built into the text.

Exam essay process

The secret of exam essay success is a good plan, which gives coverage and exploration of the title and refers to the four elements of text: plot; characterisation; language;

and themes. Think about the issues freshly rather than attempting to regurgitate your own or someone else's ideas, and avoid giving the impression of a pre-packaged essay you are determined to deliver whatever the title.

When you've chosen a question, underline its key words and define them briefly, in as many ways as are relevant to the text, to form the introduction and provide the background. Plan the rest of the essay, staying focused on the question, in approximately 12 points, recorded as short phrases and with indication of evidence. Include a concluding point which does not repeat anything already said but which pulls your ideas together to form an overview. It may refer to other readers' opinions, refer back to the title, or include a relevant quotation from the text or elsewhere.

Check your plan to see that you have dealt with all parts of the question, have used examples of the four elements of text in your support, and have analysed, not just described. Remind yourself of the Assessment Objectives (printed on the exam paper). Group points and organise the plan into a structure with numbers, brackets or arrows.

Tick off the points in your plan as you use them in the writing of your essay, and put a diagonal line through the whole plan once you have finished. You can add extra material as you write, as long as it does not take you away from the outline you have constructed.

Concentrate on expressing yourself clearly as you write your essay, and on writing accurately, concisely and precisely (e.g. 'the long vowel sounds create a mournful effect' is more specific than 'it sounds sad'). Integrate short quotations throughout the essay.

Allow 5 minutes at the end for checking and improving your essay in content and style. Insertions and crossings-out, if legible, are encouraged. As well as checking accuracy of spelling, grammar and punctuation, watch out for errors of fact, name or title slips, repetition, and absence of linkage between paragraphs. Make sure your conclusion sounds conclusive, and not as though you have run out of time, ink or ideas. A few minutes spent checking can make the difference of a grade.

Planning practice

It is a useful activity to play at being examiners and to try thinking of essay titles for planning practice. This makes you think about the main issues, some perhaps not previously considered, and which episodes would lend themselves as support for whole-text questions. Try to use the kind of language examiners use for expressing titles, which must avoid vagueness and ambiguity.

Using some of the titles below, practise planning essays within a time limit of 8 minutes, using about half a page. Aim for at least ten points and know how you would support them. Use numbers to structure the plan. Get used to using note form and abbreviations for names to save time, and to either not using your text (for closed-book examinations) or using it as little as possible.

Since beginnings are the most daunting part of the essay for many students, you could also practise opening paragraphs for your planned essays. Remember to define the terms of the title, especially any abstract words, and this will give your essay breadth, depth and structure. For example, if the word 'wartime' appears, say exactly what you take 'wartime' to mean, and how it applies to the novel you have studied.

Students also find conclusions difficult, so experiment with final paragraphs for the essays you have planned. The whole essay is working towards the conclusion, so you need to know what it is going to be before you start writing the essay, and to make it clear that you have proved your case.

Exam questions

Note that for AQA Specification A, two questions are set on each paper, one general and one extract-based.

General questions

1 Explore the ways Frayn presents uncertainty and threat during wartime.

2 Explore the ways in which characters in the novel can be considered to be 'spying'.

3 Consider the importance of the wartime setting to the effectiveness of *Spies* as a novel.

4 Consider the effectiveness of the 'dual narrator' device (old Stephen and young Stephen) in *Spies*.

5 Consider the importance of the roles played by Barbara Berrill and Mrs Hayward in Stephen's transition from child to adolescent.

6 Consider the importance and presentation of Keith in the novel.

7 Explore the ways in which Frayn presents memory and its unreliability in the novel.

8 Consider the presentation of the relationship between Stephen and Keith in the novel.

9 Explore the ways in which the themes of trust and betrayal are presented in the novel.

10 Consider the claim that *Spies* is a novel about secrets.

Extract-based questions

1 Remind yourself of the following extract from the novel. Using the extract as a starting point, consider the ways Frayn presents Keith's mother.

> She spoke softly and smilingly, with a kind of calm amusement at the world and no excessive movement of her lips. She spent a lot of the day with her feet up

on the sofa, or resting in her bedroom, and rested is how she always seemed. She'd appear in the doorway of the playroom, rested, calm, and composed, to announce that she was going down the road to Auntie Dee's, or to the shops. 'You boys will be all right, won't you? You've got things to keep you occupied?' If she wasn't going to the shops or Auntie Dee's she'd be going to the post. She posted letters, it sometimes seemed to Stephen, several times a day.

2 **Remind yourself of the following extract from the novel. Using the extract as a starting point, consider Frayn's presentation of Mr Hayward.**

Keith's father worked and worked — and as he worked he whistled. He whistled as richly and effortlessly as a songbird, an infinitely complex, meandering tune that never reached a resting place any more than his work did. He rarely found a moment to speak. When he did, the words were quick and dry and impatient. 'Door — paint — wet,' he'd inform Keith's mother. If he was in a good mood he'd address Keith as 'old chap'. Sometimes this would become 'old boy', which had imperative overtones: 'Bike away in the shed, old boy.' Occasionally, though, his lips drew back to form what appeared to be a smile, and he'd call Keith 'old bean'.

3 **Remind yourself of the following extract from the novel. Using the extract as a starting point, consider Frayn's presentation of Barbara.**

She's still looking at me, smiling secretly. She has some extra piece of knowledge that she's longing to impart.

'They kiss each other,' she whispers. 'Deirdre told me. They smoke cigarettes and then they kiss each other.'

'I know, I know,' I say, though I didn't. But I can perfectly well believe it now I do know. It's just about what Geoff *would* do.

Barbara holds the blue purse in front of her mouth, still popping and unpopping it, and looking at me over the top of it.

'Your face has gone all squidgy again,' she says.

4 **Remind yourself of the following extract from the novel. Using the extract as a starting point, consider Frayn's presentation of Keith.**

'Is Keith your best friend?' she says softly. 'Your really *really* best friend?'

I say nothing. I'm no more prepared to talk to Barbara Berrill about Keith than I am about bosoms and privets.

'Why do you like him when he's so horrible?'

I go on looking at Keith's house.

'He's so stuck-up. Everyone except you really hates him.'

Examiner notes, specimen plans and mark schemes

General questions

1 **Explore the ways Frayn presents uncertainty and threat during wartime.**

AQA examiner's comments

Successful candidates:

- explored 'uncertainty and threat', and did not neglect 'during wartime'
- approached the question from interesting angles – the car without wheels, for example, or the difficulty of buying a rabbit
- ranged across the whole novel
- explored the ways uncertainty and threat led to misinterpretation/misunderstanding of characters and events
- extended their exploration to cover the status of Stephen's family as refugees whose 'truth' is not revealed to the reader until the end
- showed themselves sensitive to the writer's use of imagery
- wrote cogently and coherently

2 **Explore the ways in which characters in the novel can be considered to be 'spying'.**

AQA mark scheme

Focus: theme of spying throughout the novel

Key words: explore, ways, characters, spying

AOs 1–3 Knowledge and understanding Clear communication Form, structure, language	AO4 Informed independent judgements	Marks and bands
■ Begins to consider <u>ways characters spy</u> and how choice of language, form and structure inform meaning ■ Supporting evidence increasingly based on close reading ■ <u>Analyses presentation of theme of spying</u> ■ Expression controlled, vocabulary widening ■ Attention to whole	■ Coherent, informed individual response to text, based on command of appropriate detail	Band 3 11–15
■ Detailed analysis and exploration of <u>theme of spying</u> ■ Critical vocabulary tellingly used	■ Mature and confident judgement ■ Clear, cogent argument	Band 4 16–20

3 Consider the importance of the wartime setting to the effectiveness of *Spies* as a novel.

Possible plan

- Introduction: *Spies* is a novel about two boys growing up in wartime. The behaviour and relationship of the boys would probably be no different in peacetime; but the wartime setting changes the context and consequences of their actions.
- At the heart of the novel are three things: the Keith–Stephen relationship; their intrusion upon the private affairs of a group of adults (who happen to include Keith's mother, father, aunt and uncle); and the tragedy of the breakdown and death of Uncle Peter.
- In general, the wartime setting lends urgency and significance to events, heightening tension. Spying on adults would be unjustifiable in peacetime; perceived wartime threats justify intrusion upon privacy.
- The Uncle Peter episode depends wholly upon the wartime setting: he would not have suffered from combat stress in peacetime; if he had a breakdown, he would receive support; he would not have been a 'hero', so there would not be such shame attached to his breakdown; he would not have had to hide away, so Dee and Bobs would not have needed to go to him in secret; he would not have felt the need to kill himself.
- Given that what the spying uncovers is the Uncle Peter situation, which depends wholly upon the wartime setting, arguably the whole power and emotion of the novel is indirectly dependent upon it.
- The wartime setting also permits additional ironies: Stephen is only in England at all because of the rise of the Nazis and their persecution of the Jews, a precursor to war; Stephen's father's status is an irony in itself; Peter's association with those who bombed and killed Stephen's relatives in Berlin is a further irony.
- Nevertheless, the relationship between Keith and Stephen, their childish games, and the interference of Barbara would all have happened in peacetime; the coming-of-age issues, the bullying and social background issues, the children–adult issues would all still have applied and been little different.
- Conclusion: although there would have been a moving and interesting novel about these children, their families and friends and a coming-of-age summer in peacetime, and there might even have been an illicit relationship between Bobs and Peter which the boys might have spied upon and found out, the novel derives most of its power and resonance from the significance added by the wartime setting and the tragedy of Uncle Peter.

Extract-based questions

1 Remind yourself of the following extract from the novel. Using the extract as a starting point, consider the ways Frayn presents Keith's mother.

She spoke softly and smilingly, with a kind of calm amusement at the world and no excessive movement of her lips. She spent a lot of the day with her feet up on the sofa, or resting in her bedroom, and rested is how she always seemed. She'd appear in the doorway of the playroom, rested, calm, and composed, to announce that she was going down the road to Auntie Dee's, or to the shops. 'You boys will be all right, won't you? You've got things to keep you occupied?' If she wasn't going to the shops or Auntie Dee's, she'd be going to the post. She posted letters, it sometimes seemed to Stephen, several times a day.

AQA examiner's comments

Successful candidates:

- maintained a clear focus on the ways Frayn presents Keith's mother
- used the extract as a starting point
- understood Stephen's perspectives both as child and adult
- tracked the writer's techniques, showing awareness of the cleverness of the dual narrative in disguising our complete understanding of Keith's mother
- traced the development of the character and the change in reader response through the novel
- explored details of her appearance and behaviour
- made perceptive comments such as: 'the scarf around Mrs Hayward's neck that echoes Stephen's bandages put the act of adultery in context' or 'Mrs Hayward represents the shifting of tides and the changing world to Stephen. Her presence conjures up themes of sensuality, beauty, betrayal, trust, and even Stephen's own loneliness'.
- wrote coherently and cogently

2 **Remind yourself of the following extract from the novel. Using the extract as a starting point, consider Frayn's presentation of Mr Hayward.**

Keith's father worked and worked — and as he worked he whistled. He whistled as richly and effortlessly as a songbird, an infinitely complex, meandering tune that never reached a resting place any more than his work did. He rarely found a moment to speak. When he did, the words were quick and dry and impatient. 'Door — paint — wet,' he'd inform Keith's mother. If he was in a good mood he'd address Keith as 'old chap'. Sometimes this would become 'old boy', which had imperative overtones: 'Bike away in the shed, old boy.' Occasionally, though, his lips drew back to form what appeared to be a smile, and he'd call Keith 'old bean'.

AQA mark scheme

Focus: whole novel

Key words: consider, presentation, Mr Hayward

AOs 1–3 Knowledge and understanding Clear communication Form, structure, language	AO4 Informed independent judgements	Marks and bands
■ Begins to consider <u>presentation</u> and how choice of language, form and structure inform meaning ■ Supporting evidence increasingly based on close reading ■ <u>Analyses presentation of Mr Hayward</u> ■ Expression controlled, vocabulary widening ■ Attention to whole	■ Coherent, informed individual response to text, based on command of appropriate detail	Band 3 11–15
■ Detailed analysis and exploration of <u>presentation of Mr Hayward</u> ■ Critical vocabulary tellingly used	■ Mature and confident judgement ■ Clear, cogent argument	Band 4 16–20

Sample essays

Below are two essays of different types, both falling within the top band. You can judge them against the Assessment Objectives for this text for your exam board and decide on the mark you think each deserves and why. You may be able to see ways in which each could be improved in terms of content, style and accuracy.

Sample essay 1: general question

Consider the presentation of the relationship between Stephen and Keith in the novel.

The relationship between the two boys, Stephen and Keith, lies at the heart of *Spies*. The decision to spy on Keith's mother, taken without any consideration of the likely consequences, led to the subsequent tragic events, but had the boys' relationship not been so strange then an innocent children's game need never have become anything else.

The reader sees the boys through the eyes of the older Stephen, an old man who has returned to the scene of his childhood trauma with a mixture of nostalgia and curiosity.

However, we are immediately alerted to his unreliability as a narrator when he says: 'No, wait. I've got that wrong.' This raises a number of key issues. Why does Stephen make a point of asserting his fallibility? And why does he not simply correct his own mistake? The implication surely is that he cannot necessarily correct all the mistakes because of failings of memory over such a length of time (more than 50 years). But this also gives the impression that old Stephen is actually 'telling' his story to an audience, rather than writing a prepared and crafted novelistic account. This warning to the reader may be taken as a more general warning about the subjectivity of what they are being offered by Stephen. Not only is his memory failing, but he remains scarred by the experiences he is retelling and, in particular, cannot be expected to be fair to Keith when the boy ended up by slitting Stephen's throat.

There are a number of other novelistic devices that make it hard for the reader to assess what happened in the Close during the war. Stephen's authorial perspective shifts unnervingly and repeatedly between the viewpoint (and, apparently, the perceptions) of young Stephen, and his adult viewpoint with the benefit of years of hindsight. It is hard to tell what Stephen thought at the time, and what is imposed retrospectively upon him by the narrator of the story.

We are first presented with Stephen and Keith in Chapter 2. Stephen is described first, and then, as if old Stephen were accompanying the boy like a ghostly shadow, we walk with him up the Close to Keith's house. It is a curious fact that we are never told the age of either boy (they must be about 12), or anything about the physical appearance of either (except for Stephen's sticking-out ears). What we are told is about clothes only. We have no idea, for example, whether Keith was older, taller, or blonder than Stephen. What we are told immediately is about their relationship: 'I see now that he was only the first in a whole series of dominant figures in my life whose disciple I became.' This tells us more about Stephen than about Keith, and is explicitly retrospective, but his other comment probably reflects Stephen's view at the time: 'He was the officer corps in our two-man army. I was the Other Ranks — and grateful to be so.' It is not just that Keith was a natural leader and Stephen a natural follower; the social chasm between them added an extra dimension of inequality: 'I was acutely aware, even then, of my incomprehensible good fortune in being Keith's friend.' It is this sense of inferiority and subservience that makes the relationship between the two boys so damaging for both of them, because it allows unlimited and unquestioned authority to someone who, it turns out, has an authoritarian personality in the first place.

The key to Keith's character is his relationship with his repressed, violent father. As the novel progresses, Keith increasingly reflects his father, rather than his gentle but duplicitous mother, adopting his clipped mannerisms and, finally, replicating his cold and unemotional violence when he cuts Stephen's throat. Very early on, we see Keith demand that Stephen swear an oath of secrecy about their spying, which Stephen willingly does; as events develop, and Stephen breaks the terms of the oath, he becomes increasingly aware of the real possibility that Keith will implement the oath's threat to impose physical harm.

Keith suggests that his mother is a German spy (the reader is never given any hint as to why this idea came into his head) and the boys duly play the make-believe game, like so many that have gone before. The difference this time, though, is that the game has consequences for real people when it turns out that Keith's mother actually does have a secret life that she has been, up to this point, successfully concealing. This is the point at which a more natural or equal relationship between the boys would have allowed them to actually talk about the situation they had got into; but Keith's contempt for Stephen, and Stephen's weak deference to Keith, prevent this conversation from ever taking place. As a result, an increasing gap opens up between the fantasy of the game and the reality of the situation, which is never discussed. Stephen, at some level, begins to acknowledge this, although it appears that Keith never does, and without taking any conscious decision to do so, Stephen begins to grow apart from Keith.

The arrival of Barbara Berrill in the hideout in the privet hedge acts as a major catalyst in many ways. She is not only an outsider; she also represents the irruption of a hitherto absent feminine dimension into Stephen's childish life. He could have simply ordered her out, but he did not, becoming instead her follower, even when it meant breaking his oath to Keith. Barbara shows Stephen a glimpse of the more adult life that awaits him if he will only break away from Keith and childish things. This new element is strengthened when Keith's mother takes him into her confidence. It is a sign of his growing maturity that he is able to empathise with her situation as an adult woman, one whom he finds attractive, and is driven further away from Keith by having more and more secrets which he must keep from him.

Keith is mysteriously absent for much of the central part of the novel, making it easier for Stephen's loyalty to him to waver and be undermined; when he comes back it is too late. Stephen has moved on in a number of ways during these summer weeks: he has smoked a symbolic cigarette with Barbara, he has made a compact of secrecy and been trusted by Mrs Hayward, and he has made his own discoveries about the 'tramp' and discovered the silk escape map. Keith, by contrast, has not developed at all, except perhaps to become an even more authoritarian clone of his father. He duly carries out the punishment by taking a knife to Stephen's throat, but what is most interesting is that he has lost his real power over him, the power of Stephen's willing submission and complicity, and now he is reduced to the mere exercise of physical power through bullying. Stephen no longer seeks or needs his approval; he has escaped from his (self-imposed) discipleship, although at considerable cost.

Old Stephen is implicitly critical of young Stephen's weakness in his initial presentation of him; although it is not said explicitly, he perhaps approves of the greater independence that Stephen achieves by the end. In the final, coda-like chapter where most of the loose ends are tied up, he says: 'I never went to Keith's house again', but this does not mean that he had entirely escaped from his spell, and when, many years later, he saw 'K. R. G. Hayward' on a door it was 'some last residual fear' that prevented him from entering. And although he asserted some independence during the fateful wartime summer, he remained a 'disciple' to 'dominant' figures throughout his life. No doubt, we are left to presume, Keith remained a bully throughout his life.

Sample essay 2: extract-based question

Remind yourself of the following extract from the novel. Using the extract as a starting point, consider Frayn's presentation of Barbara.

> She's still looking at me, smiling secretly. She has some extra piece of knowledge that she's longing to impart.
>
> 'They kiss each other,' she whispers. 'Deirdre told me. They smoke cigarettes and then they kiss each other.'
>
> 'I know, I know,' I say, though I didn't. But I can perfectly well believe it now I do know. It's just about what Geoff *would* do.
>
> Barbara holds the blue purse in front of her mouth, still popping and unpopping it, and looking at me over the top of it.
>
> 'Your face has gone all squidgy again,' she says.

The passage represents a very important stage in the developing relationship between Stephen and Barbara Berrill. Despite the significant role that she plays both in the novel and in Stephen's psychosexual development, Barbara Berrill actually only features in person three times in the whole book. Although she does not make an appearance until Chapter 5, she is introduced much earlier, in Chapter 2, in forcefully negative terms: 'Barbara Berrill, who's as sly and treacherous as most girls are.' This, of course, tells us as much about young Stephen's childish attitude as it does about Barbara, but it is significant that she is singled out for attack in this way. Clearly, this hostile first impression is designed to influence the reader's reaction when Barbara is finally encountered.

Barbara's first words when she does appear in the hideout — invading the boys' most private and secret space — are revealing: 'I knew you were playing on your own…I've got a secret way of seeing you in here.' In these two sentences she both introduces herself and establishes her methods: she seeks power through the acquisition of secret knowledge (and is therefore another of the characters in the novel involved in spying). Stephen's reaction to her uninvited arrival in their secret sanctum is 'outrage'. Nevertheless, Stephen allows her to remain and rapidly begins to fall under her spell.

The quoted passage represents the next stage. Barbara is visiting Stephen in the hideout for the third time, and it is as if she now feels she has a right to do so. Stephen has, in effect, accepted that she is his new leader, and he has become her disciple. Her hold over him derives from her invariably superior knowledge, both of what is going on in the Close and of life in general. As with all the other children, the reader is never told how old Barbara is, but she is clearly more aware of adult life than Stephen is. She has already demonstrated her uncanny awareness of goings-on of which Stephen was entirely oblivious, but now she strikes closer to home, by telling Stephen what his own brother has been getting up to with Barbara's sister. Although the source of her information is self-evident, and Stephen can immediately see how likely it is that Geoff will have been kissing Deirdre, nevertheless it is something he did not know. More tellingly, he had not even suspected it; this is partly a consequence of his distant relationship with his brother, and partly of his own fundamental naivety. When he does subsequently kiss Barbara (at her instigation, of course) he 'was too busy thinking about the germs' to notice whether it was 'nice' or not. But the passage is a clear example of Barbara's skills and intentions. The way she is 'smiling secretly' indicates the source of her power: 'some extra piece of knowledge' is what she cannot wait to impart. And when she has delivered her gem, Stephen's reaction is as it invariably is: he blusters and lies. '"I know, I know" I say, though I don't.' And she knows perfectly well that he's lying: 'Your face has gone all squidgy again', she says, reminding him of his inability to hide his reactions.

For the truth is that Barbara is not really interested in Stephen, as 'that mocking smile of her own' suggests; she probably despises him, although she may be amused at how easy it is to manipulate him. Several times Barbara says 'Didn't you know…' to reinforce her scorn at Stephen's ignorance. He is potentially useful to her, though, because he controls one of the few pieces of information about the Close that she does not already have access to: what is in the boys' locked trunk, and what exactly it is that they are doing with Mrs Hayward. Control of information is everything to Barbara, and she does eventually succeed in persuading Stephen to open the trunk and reveal its secrets. To achieve this, she employs all the wiles traditionally attributed to her sex. During her very first visit to Stephen in the hideout, he observes 'her knickers on display underneath'. Later, she offers him the opportunity to smoke his first cigarette, an experience that creates a considerably more lasting impression than the kiss: 'It tastes of importance and of being grown up', he says. However scheming Barbara may be, for Stephen she has triggered an important change: 'I see all kinds of things I never saw before.'

When Barbara first appears in the hideout, the reader is given a description of her clothes, but not of her appearance; we are therefore unable to establish, here or later, whether she is actually attractive to Stephen in any way or not. As the description proceeds, Stephen's initial distaste remains clear: 'There's something girlishly self-satisfied about the bobbliness of the leather and the shininess of the popper that offends me almost as much as her intrusion.' This, again, is a generalised criticism of girls, as Stephen perceives them, as well as an individual one of Barbara, but it is also a repetition of the observation in the quoted passage that Barbara continuously opens and closes her purse. This is a classic Freudian symbol for the vagina, and although young Stephen could hardly know that, Frayn will assume that his reader does. It may also symbolise the repository of her secrets which she is opening for him, and may reflect the traditional 'you show me yours and I'll show you mine' game of young children: she seeks access to his locked trunk and is prepared to open hers.

But with the passing of time, Stephen's overall reaction becomes equivocal: although he does not admit anything to himself, he is prepared to be led by her, at least to a certain extent, perhaps out of curiosity, perhaps out of the sheer habit of following his leader. He does not admit to finding her attractive, but she nevertheless becomes associated with a complex new set of emotions to which he attaches the evocative name 'Lamorna'. This is the name of her house, but it has a number of associations; the name itself, with its long 'o' sound, suggests

a mournful tone, and the 'La' prefix fixes it as female. It is, in fact, a place in Cornwall, with artistic connections, and the subject of a romantic song, so it is a suitable choice for a symbol of newly discovered feelings.

Barbara plays a very important role in the novel in showing Stephen the adult future that awaits him as soon as he is ready to embrace it; she has been the catalyst for his transformation from child to adolescent. She has also weakened Keith's hold over him, because even though he knows he is risking Keith's vengeance by doing so, he gives in to her blandishments and opens the trunk, breaking his solemn oath to Keith in the process. Nevertheless, once she has obtained what she seeks, her interest in him abruptly ceases. One of the saddest sentences in the book comes in the final chapter, when the elder Stephen reveals that he 'called at Lamorna several times, but Barbara could never come out to play.' She had no real interest in Stephen, as he found out the hard way.

Overall then, the presentation of Barbara (by the elder Stephen, of course, with the benefit of hindsight) is interestingly balanced: it shows her fascination, skill and power, and how Stephen fell helplessly under her spell; but it never makes her seem anything other than manipulative and, in the end, indifferent to Stephen.

Further study

There are many books about Britain during the Second World War. The most recent is *Wartime: Britain 1939–1945* by Juliet Gardiner (2004, paperback 2005), a highly readable account based principally upon personal testimony. On the RAF bombing campaign against Germany, see http://www.bbc.co.uk/history/worldwars/wwtwo/air_war_bombers_01.shtml

No books of criticism have yet been published on *Spies*; this is not uncommon for modern fiction, and the bulk of the critical responses available are in the form of reviews of the novels. A good starting point is http://www.complete-review.com/reviews/fraynm/spies.htm, which has comprehensive links to all the published reviews of the novel, as well as various sites about Frayn. An interview published in the *Guardian* newspaper (which may be found at http://books.guardian.co.uk/departments/generalfiction/story/0,6000,642272,00.html) includes some useful biographical background information.

http://www.fantasticfiction.co.uk/authors/Michael_Frayn.htm includes useful material, as does http://www.contemporarywriters.com/authors/?p=auth114.

Film version

There is a project to film *Spies*, but it is not, at the time of writing, very far advanced; it is known that Michael Frayn is writing the screenplay himself and it will be directed by his daughter, Rebecca.